To Tony—thanks for marrying into the family. You are a great son-in-law.
To Christy and John, the best kids a father could have.
—James

To Adonai, thank you. To Misty, thank you for always putting up with my latest emergency and
for always being there. To Nikolas, Matthew, and Jakob—it is my honor to say you are my sons.
—Ervin

CYBERSECURITY

BRIDGING THE GAP BETWEEN TECHNICIAN & MANAGEMENT

Kendall Hunt
publishing company

James R. Phelps ■ Ervin Frenzel

Cover image © Shutterstock.com

Kendall Hunt
publishing company

www.kendallhunt.com
Send all inquiries to:
4050 Westmark Drive
Dubuque, IA 52004-1840

Copyright © 2017 by Kendall Hunt Publishing Company

ISBN 978-1-5249-2196-5

Published in the United States of America

BRIEF CONTENTS

CONTENTS

ACKNOWLEDGMENTS

First, we must acknowledge the Cyber Engineering faculty at Texas Tech University. They included Angelo State Homeland Security faculty in their National Science Foundation grant application and that process brought Ervin and James together through a series of workshops funded under NSF Award #1241578. However, no federal funding was used to create this work. Additionally, we need to thank our students from all fields of study that routinely brought to our attention the problems they faced in talking and working with geeks or managers. It is a tough situation the Internet and cyber science has created, resulting in differentiated thought processes and languages amongst those wishing to accomplish the same ends.

From Kendall Hunt Publishing we thank Angela Willenbring, our Senior Developmental Coordinator for all her hard work in keeping us focused, working with us as deadlines passed, and helping us to get the final product to the printers. We also need to thank Karen Fleckenstein, our project manager, she did a wonderful work arranging the book you are reading. Without her we'd have been lost! Of course, without the introduction to Paul Carty at ACJS in March of 2016, and the interest he showed in getting this book started, we would have never felt moved to fill such an obvious gap in the available literature.

On a personal note, no such undertaking as difficult as a book can be accomplished without the support of our families and friends. While we cannot possibly remember everybody that helped, offered support, or ideas, none of you should feel slighted by not being mentioned. We thank all of you for the big ideas—and the small points—without which we could not have found the time nor motivation to carry this through to completion. Misty, Nikolas, Matthew, and Jakob were essential to our putting ideas into words. Thank you all for helping, sustaining, and motivating us behind the scenes as life constantly moved and changed the world around us. Anthony "Tony" Anzelmo—you are a CYBER GOD—and we are glad you were available to offer advice and editing on the parts we struggled with and concepts that were difficult to address. And to Dr. Muhammad Afzaal, thank you for always shaking my (James) hand, treating this social scientist and historian with respect, and answering my questions while I jumped into your field of study. This type of support cannot be measured nor effectively acknowledged in words.

ABOUT THE AUTHORS

James Phelps, PhD, received his doctorate in Criminal Justice from Sam Houston State University (2008). He is a graduate of FEMA's National Emergency Management Advanced (and Basic) Academies; the U.S. Navy's Radiological Controls Officer and Nuclear Planners school in Charleston, South Carolina. He has taught history for the NCPACE Afloat program taking college classes to sailors deployed at sea, often in dangerous locals. James developed the graduate and under-graduate online Border and Homeland Security degrees at Angelo State University, and was the majority contributor to their graduate program in Criminal Justice, all top-10 ranked nationally in their fields of study. He teaches cybersecurity online for NOVA Southeastern's Department of Emergency Management graduate program as well as many other courses across the world. Most importantly, he is the primary mover and developer of the first Security and Strategic Studies Doctorate program offered in the Middle East, at American University in the Emirates, in Dubai, UAE. Dr. Phelps is a 100 percent disabled veteran currently living and working from his home in the Colorado Rocky Mountains where he conducts research, writes, and occasionally teaches as he feeds hummingbirds and enjoys nature's beauty.

Ervin Frenzel, MISM, received his Master's Degree from University of Phoenix online as well is pursuing a DOM/IST. He holds multiple IT and Management certifications including the CISSP, HCISPP, ECSA, CEH, CIH, A+, Network +, Security +, HIT, Cloud Essentials, and MCITP. Ervin spent almost ten years in the intelligence field for the US Army, where he developed a love of working with people and technology and combining the two. He initially designed the Networking/Cybersecurity Program (A.A.S.) for Amarillo College. He teaches online security courses for both Amarillo College (Amarillo, Texas) and North Central Texas College (Corinth, Texas campus). He currently works full-time as a networking and security administrator for a major US city and continues to study, write, and teach online courses.

PREFACE

The Internet isn't a place. The Cloud isn't a thing. Growing up with technology doesn't mean understanding it. Each of these plain statements is true and horribly misleading without substantial additional information. I have spent a career explaining technology and the way humans interact with it. I have a very keen sense of just how complicated some of these topics can get. I sometimes think that learning about security through the inner workings of computers is like trying to learn Latin from historic law books. It is unreasonably hard without good explanation. You need to understand both the language and the reality that the language describes to really get it.

In this book, James Phelps and Ervin Frenzel look at a wide variety of particularly selected topics from the perspective of a reasonably intelligent person interacting with a brand new language and thought process. He uses select topics to teach not just language of computer security, but some of the fundamental concepts and most importantly, he lays the foundation for why it is necessary. This is not simply a simplified introduction to computer security text. It is not a survey of all of the meaningful security concepts. It is a basis upon which an interested and attentive reader can build a meaningful understanding of a complex and incredibly important subject.

WHY SIMPLIFICATIONS ARE SIMPLY NOT GOOD ENOUGH

The Internet is a method of communication, not a place. It is easy to get lost in the analogies used to simplify this extremely complex method. Law enforcement has learned over the years how difficult it is to locate actors on the Internet. It can be very complex to understand which laws govern communication on the Internet. Nigerian Princes extract money from hapless victims and cannot be found or charged. On the other, people engaging in perfectly legal activities in their home may be subject to prosecution around the world. Blasphemy laws from halfway around the world can be applied to free speech. Prohibitions on Nazi memorabilia or holocaust denial, political speech under repressive regimes, or anything found odious by those with the power to make law—right or wrong. World travelers can be stopped at the border and have their passwords demanded to access their activities on the Internet. In the United States, it is unclear whether the results are sufficient for criminal prosecution or simply for denial of entry. However legal an Internet activity may be under the law of where it occurs, there can be meaningful consequences elsewhere.

"The" Cloud is a masterpiece of technology oversimplification. When someone says "The" Cloud I mentally translate it to "other people's servers." The beauty of it is that the Cloud has freed technicians of the need to explain things to their managers. Inevitably, this goes wrong. Security suffers, unforeseen trade-offs become very present, the disadvantages to putting other people in control of your data become very apparent. One aspect of the Cloud that managers are just beginning to understand is that other people's servers come with risk. Availability is guaranteed by the provider and in the vast majority of cases, it works. What happens when the provider goes out of business? Does the data owner get reasonable warning to remove their data from that cloud? Can it simply be "Cloud-magically" moved to another provider's cloud and what does that service look like or cost? What happens when the courts order access to data and metadata that describes how and where the data is stored? Can a manager or corporate counsel explain, in court, how that type of data simply doesn't exist? What if the court orders data to be permanently deleted because it is found to belong to someone else or was collected in a way that violates privacy laws? Google doesn't know how many copies it keeps of that data or where.

We hear that young people today have grown up with technology. There is a tremendous increase in the sophistication of the use of technology from one generation to the next, but that doesn't grant an understanding of the technology. As an analogy, many people can drive a car. Far fewer can explain and repair an engine, hydraulic system, electronic ignition system, or in some cases change a tire. Securing computers and networks requires some fairly detailed knowledge about the precise way data is processed at the destination of a transmission. Many of the sophisticated users of today recognize a green "locked" icon and even the name of a certifying authority means that a connection is secure. Far fewer recognize that the certificates behind that trusted connection may have been stolen and used to impersonate a reputable company. It is often hard for sophisticated users to get over their understanding and the assumptions that go with it. The user interface has become so good and the system has become so intuitive, that the simplifications have become reality to many users.

To effectively investigate crimes or secure these systems, we must understand the underlying reality. The book in your hands (or on your e-reader/phone/screen) helps us to start the conversation that demystifies the underlying details that make computers and networks function. This book is not the final word in the conversation, but it undoes a lot of over-simplifications like the ones stated above.

WHEN GOOD TECHIES WRITE BAD MATERIAL

I once wrote a nice piece for an encyclopedia about computer forensics using an example that walked step-by-step through commands and explained what each one did. I explained how irreducible the method was; it allowed no argument because it examined and interpreted the data at a level of detail that is directly equivalent to looking at the ones and zeros. I showed how to look at data formatting to reveal details hidden from investigators who just used software. In all, I was proud of how neat and tidy it turned out. When I finally saw it in print, I realized how horribly wrong I was. It was in an encyclopedia of criminal justice. While everything I wrote was true and on topic, I lost track of the context. To carry on the analogy above, I had written a grammatically perfect piece of Latin describing sheep-pen easements before William the Conqueror took England. It couldn't have been more obscure in that context.

When I interact with people, I can see their confusion and ask them questions about their level of knowledge. I regularly adjust my presentations to my audience and either go deeper into the technical details or stick to broad explanations. Without this feedback, I can embarrass myself by appearing too superficial for technical people or too hopelessly obscure for non-technical people. Sadly, even the ones in the middle can object to a presentation because it doesn't target their direct interests.

James Phelps and Ervin Frenzel have written this book to address one particular mission: to break down communication barriers between technically trained people and non-technically trained people. It presents a wide variety of technical topics relevant to many of the situations found in modern security discussions. It does not benefit from direct feedback from the reader as you progress. At times a reader may lack the background to fully appreciate why a topic is presented. Another reader might find the approach in one area too basic. However, in general this book attempts to hold true to the stated purpose of explaining an immensely complex subject that comes with many partisans willing and eager to express their opinions on exactly how each topic should be explained.

AN OVERVIEW, NOT AN OVER SIMPLIFICATION

It is impossible to cover every topic in computer security in a meaningful way in one book, or even a series of books. Instead, Jim selects topics that lead to deeper understanding over the current buzzwords. I have seen many buzzwords and new technologies come and go. To illustrate this, I once bought some very expensive forensic gadgets. To protect them I bought a Pelican Case.™ You have probably seen these in airports or if you were in the military. They are hard plastic, incredibly durable protective boxes with water-resistant seals. I recently gave the forensic gadgets to an electronics recycler. I still use the Pelican Case. If you build a solid understanding of technology and how the fundamentals interact, you can always put the latest gadget in there. Change the label to the new buzzword and you are ready to hit the marketplace as an up-to-date security professional.

IN THIS BOOK

It is easy to simply assume that computer security is important, but the details can be very important in assigning priorities to threats and understanding the risks that computer security efforts address. Chapter 1 introduces the playing field and begins an analysis of the relative power of broad groups of actors in computer security. Chapter 2 deepens this effort by explaining classic elements of security and the power structure (laws) that support security efforts. Chapter 3 focuses on the concrete issue of data privacy by introducing how data is stored and then introducing encryption. Without some of these fundamentals it is hard to understand how and why encryption works to secure data.

Chapter 4 enriches the basic security information with threats. Various crimes and attacks are explained in a level of detail appropriate to the established understandings presented in previous chapters. With sufficient motivation prompted by an understanding of the threats found in Chapter 4, Chapter 5 explains encryption both at a functional level and as a building block for security. This chapter explains several different uses of encryption without getting sidetracked by marketing hype or mathematical theory.

Chapter 6 starts to get into details of how networks operate. Just like file systems and data storage allowed a discussion of encryption, dynamic transfer of data on a network sets up a deeper discussion of security theory. Chapter 6 also includes its own concrete look at network activity that can be used for crime. Chapter 7 drives much more deeply into the details of how computers and software interact to explain how software vulnerabilities work. Again, the emphasis is on a basic understanding that helps explain why these vulnerabilities exist and how they are generally approached from a security standpoint. Chapter 8 looks at attacks using network services. The chapter describes attacks and threats through applications like e-mail and web browsers, but also looks at the underlying details of how the application uses network services. This gives the reader insight into investigating and securing these threats and attacks. Chapter 9 deepens the approach of understanding basic network services and illustrates these points with concrete examples like the functions of TOR and the Dark Web.

Chapter 10 refocuses the reader on threats posed by malicious actors and the limits of technical security in a world where real people use computers. The chapter uses real-world threats from insiders to social engineering to bypass technical security. Chapter 11 examines the structures that guide human behavior. The chapter examines the effects of laws seeking to control malicious behavior or striving to strike a balance between protection and legitimate use and privacy. The book ends with a call to action in Chapter 12, but stays true to form in that it introduces material showing and explaining the consequences of our inaction.

CONCLUSION

This broad approach is well suited to management classes and for anyone required to grapple with the broad concepts of information security. It will work well in introduction classes supporting a broad survey of security topics to familiarize the reader with some meaning behind the buzzwords. As stated before, this book is not a dry but comprehensive high level survey of information security knowledge domains. It is not infotainment drawn primarily from journalistic sources with incomplete comprehension of the underlying topic. It is a tool to understand information security well enough to communicate with people who do understand it deeply. It is a guide to the topic that establishes enough understanding to make informed choices about what to learn next. It is a start.

Dr. D. Kall Loper, PhD
LoperForensics.com
20 April 2017

CHAPTER 1

INTRODUCTION TO INFORMATION SECURITY: THE NEED FOR SECURITY

KEY WORDS

Asymmetries of Power
Lack of Borders

Problem of Anonymity
World Wide Web (WWW)

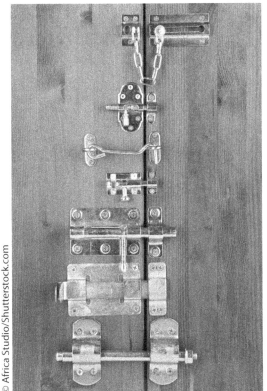

© Africa Studio/Shutterstock.com

WE WOULDN'T LEAVE HOME WITHOUT LOCKING THE DOORS? WOULD WE?

Most of us, when we walk away from our homes we check to ensure that the doors are closed and locked. We close and lock the windows too. If we do leave a window or two cracked open, then we usually have some sort of locking mechanism to ensure that the window can't be opened far enough to allow access to either the locking device or the interior of the house. We also make sure our garage door is closed or at least down nearly to the ground.

We have any number of locks on our doors. The main exterior doors often have deadbolt locks as well and sometimes even chains and other devices. We often go to excessive lengths to ensure our homes and apartments are protected from unwanted intruders.

Unfortunately, we are all faced with the prospect that somebody will want to get into our homes to take something of ours, or personally threaten us and our

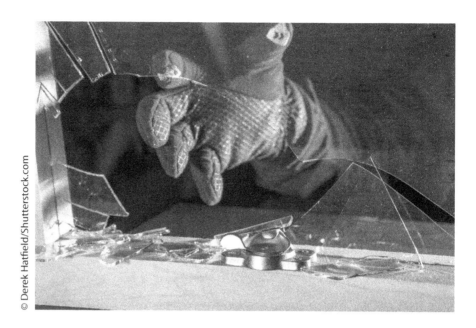

© Derek Hatfield/Shutterstock.com

family. Sometimes, no matter what we do, the thief will do more, even breaking through our barriers to get to what we have and want to protect.

What we have to decide is to what length we go to protect what's ours? We could all live in underground caves, with barred and locked doors, but in doing so we will be giving away our access to light and scenery, views, and emergency egress in event of a disaster. Our homes would be wet, humid, possibly even moldy, and much of what we do have would be subject to loss from causes other than thievery.

© Sergiy Palamarchuk/Shutterstock.com

The same problem exists for our data, software, information sources, networks, and communications. We don't want somebody listening in on a private conversation with our spouse or lover any more than we want somebody in the room taking notes when we discuss our investments with our financial advisor. Even the US Congress has a secure room where proposed legislation of a highly sensitive or classified nature can be reviewed by legislators and select members of their staffs without being in the public eye. Yet we all do things every day that puts our information and communications at risk of exposure to competitors, thieves, and others we wouldn't want to be able to see, read, or hear what we are doing or have done.

That's one of the reasons for this book—understanding the security needs of our agencies, corporations, and homes. Not from the perspective of the "expert" but from the perspective of those that manage the Information Technology or Information Security department. We want you to be able to understand what types of locks and chains are on your computer and network systems and to be able to speak with and understand what the experts are talking about when they come to you with a concern, a report of a penetration, or even to tell you that all your data and your identity has been stolen.

WE CAN'T BE AN EXPERT IN EVERYTHING

We need our technicians. They need their managers. It is a symbiotic relationship essential to the organization. In the case of information technology technicians, their ability to communicate with management is virtually impossible because the tech and manager do not speak the same language. One talks about bytes, RAM, SQL, and the other hears lunch, sheep, and something wiggly. Neither do the directions of management translate well to the technician.

In organizations that are purely tech based, pretty much everybody outside the business and human resources offices speak the same language. In government and most other businesses the IT tech shop is just another component of organizational operations. Just as engineers in the *Dilbert* comic strip can't communicate with sales or human resources, we often have difficulty communicating with our IT techs and they can't communicate with us.

This is a second reason for this book—to provide the manager with the language skills to communicate effectively with their IT shop.

We can't all be experts in everything. The true Jack-of-All-Trades that is skilled in every aspect of an organization is very rare. We specialize all the time and become experts in one area, or perhaps two. But never all the areas. So being able to communicate across specializations is essential, particularly in this cyber world where business is done at the speed of light across the entire world and into space—and threats are no longer just at our doors, but attack us from half a world away.

IS CYBERSECURITY REALLY A PROBLEM?

It sure is! Not just a problem with crime, but now with nation-states as actors learning and practicing how to disrupt critical infrastructure operations, industrial and government espionage, massive bank thefts on a scale never seen or imagined, and even the manipulation of stock markets. People steal the identity of other people, create credit cards in their names, and make purchases of tens of thousands of dollars in their names. Other people simply put a virus on a million individual computers that puts up a fake FBI page that locks their computers—requiring payment of a couple hundred dollars to get the unlock code. If this happens to your business are you calling the police or paying the money and then calling the police? What if you are the police? Then what do you do?

What if you are in an industry where your sensitive equipment must operate within a very narrow band and if it runs too fast, too slow, too hot, or too cold it breaks, wears out early, or simply produces a bad product that you can't sell? That would probably be very bad for the company and its customers who may be the first to discover the actual problem. Sound scary? It should. This is what the STUXNET program accomplished at the Iranian uranium enrichment plant.

In the late 1990s I worked at a chemical manufacturing company where we made a product called tungsten hexa-fluoride, used in etching silicon wafers in computer chip manufacturing plants. Very corrosive and highly flammable, the product had to have no hydrogen in it and we loaded it into compressed gas cylinders either made of or lined with pure nickel. Only we had a problem—batch after batch was contaminated with hydrogen. No matter how clean the cylinders, or how carefully we monitored the process, all the tests came back contaminated. We couldn't figure it out for over two months. We calibrated the test equipment over and over. We disassembled whole sections of the manufacturing process and completely rebuilt it. We couldn't solve the problem and I moved on to another company before the issue was resolved. I later visited and talked with my former co-workers and found out that the problem wasn't us! It was the calibration gas used

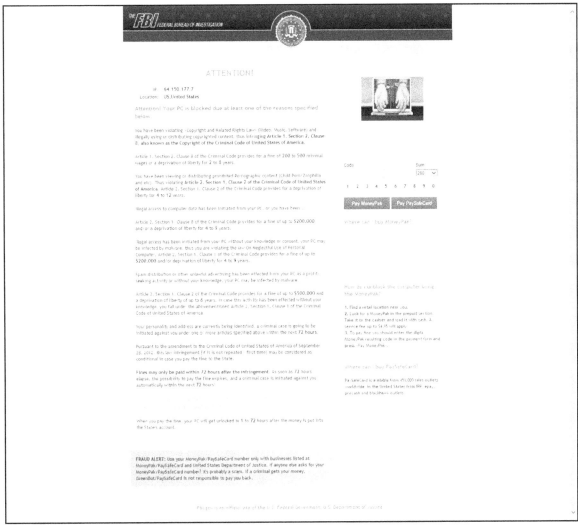

Screenshot of FBI Ransomware produced by CRYPTOKEY.

in the test device. Somebody at another plant had filled a helium cylinder with hydrogen gas, and sent it to us. The gas we were using to purge and calibrate the test instruments was contaminating the equipment and providing false sample results. Yet that cylinder was clearly marked and tagged as being helium. That simple mistake nearly closed the plant, cost the jobs of several workers and managers, ruined reputations for quality, and endangered not only the workers, but the neighboring community. Imagine if that was to happen to something critical at your place of business? Could your company or agency survive a two- to three-month period where you dumped product not because the product was bad but because the test equipment incorrectly told you the product was bad? Today, with the presence of malware like STUXNET on the web, this can happen to anybody in any business.

Consider the earlier case of identity theft and locked computers. Who is the larger problem? The person that steals your identity and makes several thousands of dollars in fake purchases? Or the person who steals $200 from a million people yet never once commits a crime that rises above petty theft in most jurisdictions?

Personally, as authors of this book we are thinking of creating a malware program that gets you to pay us $50 every time you click on a link. . . . We need to fund our entertainment budget some way!

If you are reading this on an electronic device,

CLICK HERE

WHAT IS WWW?

WORLD WIDE WEB
An interconnected web of servers that simply switch packets of information around the globe.

The World Wide Web (**WWW**) is nothing more than an interconnected web of servers that simply switch packets of information around the globe. I wrote this chapter in Dubai, in the United Arab Emirates, using a MacBook Pro laptop computer. I sent it to my co-author in Dallas, Texas, USA. In that process the chapter was scanned multiple times by virus and anti-spam software before leaving my computer and upon receipt at his computer and by several servers that host Google Mail programs. The chapter was then edited and sent back to me via e-mail. The packet of information containing the chapter file passed through a number of computers including:

104.47.42.119
25.173.146.132
10.202.177.6
10.176.6.67
10.168.238.13
10.168.238.15
15.1.734.8
15.01.0734.014

These are called IP addresses and are the specific and unique numbers assigned to computers. Each one that handled a part of the transmission of the data packet that included this chapter, images, and e-mail content was required to leave its own identifier as part of the routing process. If you wanted to, you could look up each of these IPs and see where each is located and who owns them. We might just do that in a later chapter.

At any point along the transmission route a capture program might have collected the images and files attached to the e-mail and tried to examine them. It's likely that was done on the way into and out of the UAE (the government monitors everything), however I'm not sure if it happened along the rest of the route. In any case, you now know what the WWW is. We get into greater detail in a later chapter.

DUMB AND SMART MACHINES

The MacBook Pro laptop I typed this chapter on is a dumb machine. It does exactly what I tell it to do. At no point, will this machine suddenly turn on and start operating all by itself and type the chapters of the next book I write. Nor will it suddenly decide to turn on or off the lights in my office. It has the capability to do both but still requires operator input.

Sometime soon humans will create a thinking and learning machine that is self-aware. We call that type of machine Artificial Intelligence or AI. Since we haven't yet reached the point where AI is running everything for us, we still should look at the computers we use as electric information processors that require operator input. The "smart" behind these types of machines are the people that operate them. What you will find out is that most of those operating computers aren't all that smart and while we can program software to scan and identify e-mail for threats, autocorrect spelling errors, and complete typed entries based on models of what we have previously typed, the computer still fundamentally does exactly what it is told.

The real intelligence in our computers is at the edge of our system, in our smartphones and laptops, running various "apps" or application programs. Apps can monitor our health, tell us we've been sitting too long, calculate how far we have walked, measure the air quality we breathe and warn us when the dust or pollen level is going to cause an asthma attack, and even communicate with our doctor when we aren't well. These apps are installed on our devices when we tell the device to connect to a server and download the programming.

Sometimes programs that we want to install have other script attached or embedded that will do bad things to our computers, such as lock our screen and tell us we have to send the FBI $200 to get an unlock code. This is where we get into trouble and find ourselves in need of the IT people at work or at home—usually because the computer operator wasn't as smart as they should have been.

Maybe AI and Skynet aren't all that bad after all . . .

VULNERABILITIES

The Internet is huge. There are billions of web pages that are currently active and nearly half the world population has ready access to them. People are creating new web pages and registering new domain names at a rate of more than one per second. All of this creates a massive and expansive source of information that is open to just about everybody.

The way the Internet is built, anyone with a new idea can design that idea in a way that it can be posted to the Internet through purchase of a Domain Name and renting some server space. There are even programs that will design and build you a basic website automatically. Once built, virtually any function can be added to that website—an online store, a virtual game, music files, videos, or a government database. It is this flexibility that has driven the explosive growth of the web.

Unfortunately, this creates a door to vulnerabilities.

PROBLEM OF ANONYMITY

A person can claim to be anybody when creating a web page and putting information into it; there is no verification that you are who you claim.

The first vulnerability is the **problem of anonymity**. You can claim to be anybody when you create that web page and put information into it. Nobody verifies that you are who you claim. So, you could be George Washington, or John Adams, or Thomas Jefferson, or James Phelps, or Ervin Frenzel, and you could even be another Ervin Frenzel or James Phelps than the ones writing this book. Yet when it comes to the web nobody can tell you that you aren't that particular person.

A second vulnerability is the difficulty in distinction between the different types of cyber activity. Code is code. All code is basically similar and on the front end the code looks very similar. This is how hackers can hide code inside other programs your computer is using.

ASYMMETRIES OF POWER

The third vulnerability inherent in the Internet; with over three billion people connected, there is much room for those who want to interrupt service or attack corporations or governments.

The nature of the Internet creates enhanced **asymmetries of power**. This is the third vulnerability inherent in the Internet. With over 3 billion people connected to the Internet; Google (by far the largest search engine in use today) processing over 40,000 unique searches every second and over 1.2 trillion searches per year worldwide; 1.79 billion Facebook monthly active users generating over 4.5 billion "likes" every day; and over 205 billion e-mails sent each and every day, the Internet is a busy place. Being able to control even a small part of the process is profitable, but also opens a door for those who want to cause service interruptions or attack certain corporations or governments.

LACK OF BORDERS

A vulnerability of the Internet; the web is globalized and this creates a major problem when a crime is committed, terrorists use the web, or nation-states launch cyber-attacks on other nation-states.

The last of the vulnerabilities we are all exposed to on the Internet is the **lack of borders**. The web is globalized. Even complete isolationist countries like North Korea have Internet access of some sort. This creates a major problem with jurisdiction when crime is committed, or terrorists use the web, or nation-states launch cyber-attacks on other nation-states.

PROTECTING OUR DATA

All this activity means we need to establish a system to protect what we have from those that want it. We do this with firewalls, spam and ad blockers, white lists and black lists, and constantly updated anti-virus programs. Yet, the enemy still gets to us and takes our data or compromises our computers. In today's world, with all the protections that are available, the place we are most vulnerable are in the people we employ that use our systems and data every day.

Edward Snowden is an excellent example of what happens when people share their secure login information. According to a 2013 *Reuters* article by Mark Hosenball and Warren Strobel,

> Former U.S. National Security Agency contractor Edward Snowden used login credentials and passwords provided unwittingly by colleagues at a spy base in Hawaii to access some of the classified material he leaked to the media, sources said. . . . Snowden may have persuaded between 20 and 25 fellow workers at the NSA regional operations center in Hawaii to give him their logins and passwords by telling them they were needed for him to do his job as a computer systems administrator, a second source said (2013).

We all have Snowdens' in our workplace. We don't know when or if they will hit a breaking point, but people do hit that point and sometimes they act out against a perceived target. We see workplace violence, active shooters, assaults, sabotage of equipment or delivery systems all around the world. Today—in addition to the usual concerns of management with employees in some circles, this can be thought of as insider threat, the person we need to be careful of is the tech that has access to our deepest secrets. They can cause the most damage by far. Yet they are not the only ones.

At one of my previous employers we had an Office Coordinator that had to have a new computer every month. The reason—she destroyed one each month because no matter how many times she was told, trained, or reprimanded, when she wasn't actively employed with work she was on Facebook, YouTube, and other sites clicking on anything and everything that she saw or that somebody sent her or shared via social media or e-mail. She never understood that just opening a link, clicking on an ad, or viewing a photo or video could concurrently embed a virus or malware in her computer. Within a few days the computer was acting up. Within a week it needed major IT attention. By the end of the month it had become unrecoverable.

I know—you have policies in place to prevent this at your workplace. You have rules and protocols and your IT people will shut down somebody doing these activities. You have firewalls and scan programs to keep these types of outside attacks from getting into your system. You probably even have a policy that says you can terminate somebody for accessing social media and personal e-mail on a company computer. So did my employer. So does the Nuclear Regulatory Commission. The NRC Inspector General reported, "that from fiscal 2013 to 2014, NRC saw an 18 percent increase in computer security incidents reported to the Department of Homeland Security, such as unauthorized access, malicious code, social engineering, policy violations, scans and probes. The number was almost double the 9.7 percent increase in attacks government wide during the same period." If the folks that regulate nuclear power in the United States has this sort of problem, what makes you think you and your organization don't have this problem?

WHO POLICES THE INTERNET?

The authors are not really certain who polices the Internet. There are laws against certain activities and they have evolved from the traditional criminal law and government applies these laws to Internet crime. When a crime is committed on the Internet, the investigation depends on a number of points including who has jurisdiction. Did the crime cross jurisdictional boundaries? What about international boundaries (which it almost always does)? Was the criminal act actually criminal in the country where the perpetrator resides? What about the other countries that might have been crossed by the Internet links that facilitated the commission of the crime, are those ISPs, servers, and routers and their owners and operators culpable? All these questions are asked each and every time somebody commits a criminal act on the web. In almost all cases law enforcement has to make a number of additional determinations including if an investigation meets the cost/benefit ratio to make a formal investigation appropriate. Most Internet crimes simply do not reach that threshold.

THE OUTLINE

Realizing that there are innumerable problems facing those that work in IT and those that manage IT operations, we thought it would benefit both groups if somebody could break down the communication barriers between them. We could have written a book for the technicians to help them communicate with management. However we saw a real need in getting traditional organizations to work the communication process in the other direction. Our current organizations are much like our infrastructure, built and maintained using technology that is decades or even centuries old. Rather than trying to fit the new technology into an old world we saw the real benefit would be to take the older systems and provide a lexicon that would help them understand and communicate with the new.

We open with just that, a lexicon of computer-speak. If you don't know the language you won't understand the need. We follow that with some understanding of what we actually use computers to do, from generation of data to securing that data through encryption. Not only is encryption needed to help protect us from cybercrime, it allows us to keep spies (industrial, criminal, and national) at bay.

Next we move into the realm of using computers in series and parallel to increase our power and resources. From there we move into the concepts of how that increase in power and capability to communicate also increases our vulnerabilities. Not everything we look at or access is safe. Nor is everything we are sent actually from those who claim to be people or companies we know and trust. There is a lot of good in a globalized Internet and ready access to information. There are also bad actors out there that have other motives. If you believe that what you see when you conduct a Google search is a lot of information, you're about to find out that 80 percent of the web isn't readily searchable. The web has its dark areas, deep areas, and layered areas that make it difficult to impossible to determine who is doing what.

We close the text with a review of the most dangerous component of the cyber world—people. Not the bad actors that will always be out there—but us! We tend to be our own worst enemies when it comes to security and it doesn't matter if we are private individuals or the government. There is always some data or software we don't want others to see or find. How we do that is up to us and the level of encryption and protection we place around us. Unfortunately, as long as that information exists there will be those who want to get access to it if just to cause embarrassment.

CONCLUSION

As with the fundamental point about securing our homes when we walk away at the beginning of this chapter, when it comes to the Internet we are responsible to ensure our systems and data are secure. In the 2016 US Presidential Elections the Democratic National Committee was hacked.

Russians were blamed, accused, and asked to do even more by the opposition. Who hacked the DNC may be less important than the impact the revealed information had on the voters.

One of the Presidential candidates was found to have a private server, used to conduct work-related business when she was in the government, including the sending and receiving of national security information and classified data. There were denials, reprisals, surreptitious meetings between ex-presidents and attorney generals, statements and testimony before Congress by the director of the FBI, and still nobody was charged for the crimes committed. Asking the question "Why" might be less important than asking the question "Why Not." Ultimately it comes down to the need for secrecy. The government needs some secrecy in its operations and communications. So too does law enforcement, business, and private individuals.

Ensuring that secrecy and maintaining our privacy and that of our agencies and organizations is one of the primary reasons for this book. We want you, the reader, to be able to efficiently and effectively communicate with your IT technicians. To do that you need to be able to comprehend the language involved in this new and evolving cyber world.

QUESTIONS FOR FURTHER CONSIDERATION

1. How is cybercrime reminiscent of traditional crime?

2. How has the Internet made criminal activity easier?

3. How has the Internet made criminal activity more difficult?

4. The largest and the smallest organizations are susceptible to criminal activity. What are some of the activities that an employer should be leery of? Fellow employees?

5. Describe insider threat, at your workplace and then at your home. Is one more dangerous than the other or are both equally as dangerous? Why do you believe your answer is correct?

REFERENCES

Hosenball, Mark and Warren Strobel. 2013. "Exclusive: Snowden persuaded other NSA workers to give up passwords—sources." *Reuters* (November 7). http://www.reuters.com/article/net-us-usa-security-snowden-idUSBRE9A703020131108.

Rockwell, Mark. 2016. "'Good enough' isn't good enough to secure NRC network center." FCW, The Business of Federal Technology (January 14). https://fcw.com/articles/2016/01/14/nrc-cyber-rockwell.aspx

CHAPTER 2

BUILDING A COMMON LEXICON: UNDERSTANDING SECURITY AND COMPUTERS

KEY WORDS

Availability	Information Security	Scope of Work
Computer	Information	Terminal Mainframe
Confidentiality	Technology	Network
Field Engineer	Integrity	

INFORMATION TECHNOLOGY

COMPUTER
Programmable, usually electronic device that can store, retrieve, and process data.

So first things first what is a **computer**? What is (**information) technology**? And worse what is (information) security? What role does it really play for an organization? These questions seem like they are pretty obvious, but they really aren't. They mean different things depending upon who you are talking to.

To highlight this let me explain, a comptroller for a car dealership was having a new network installed, it was fantastic, her organization was going from a terminal and mainframe system to a windows based network. In a **terminal mainframe network**, all work that a user does is performed on the mainframe itself and it is simply reflected on the terminal screen. In a windows based network, the computers are capable of performing tasks without needing another computer to do the work. As the regional **Field Engineer** (FE) covering the location of the car dealership, I was charged

INFORMATION TECHNOLOGY

Any equipment or interconnected system or subsystem of equipment that is used in the automatic acquisition, storage, manipulation, management, movement, control, display, switching, interchange, transmission, or reception of data or information by the executive agency. The term information technology includes computers, ancillary equipment, software, firmware and similar procedures, services (including support services), and related resources.

TERMINAL MAINFRAME NETWORK

Computers used primarily by large organizations for critical applications, bulk data processing, such as census, industry, and consumer statistics, enterprise resource planning, and transaction processing.

FIELD ENGINEER

Technician charged with design, implementation, support, and maintenance of the networks within their region.

© pikcha/Shutterstock.com

with design, implementation, support, and maintenance of the networks within my region. Months of preparation had gone into the design, including the migration plan for the databases, replacement of terminals, printers, network hubs (now moving to network switches), placement of a Microsoft print server, and installation/integration of a network router to bring Internet access into the organization.

I had previously replaced the network equipment, installed and mapped many of the new printers, and all that was needed at this point was the migration of the databases. I had even prepositioned the PC's for easy cutover. During the night of the conversion I worked feverishly, switched over forty terminals with Personal Computers (PC's), migrated all of the information from their mainframe to the new windows server and had everything ready to go at 7 a.m. the next morning. I worked with the service drive advisors and demonstrated what was needed, then the parts department personnel on how to work within their specific areas, and finally I worked with sales and accounting. The final two that would need assistance were of course the comptroller and the general manager, both of which owned a portion of the dealership that I was working with so neither needed to be there when the rest of the dealership opened.

The dealership had now been open for three hours, I was exhausted and everything seemed to be flowing as intended. I loaded up my tools, and headed back to my house for some well-deserved rest, or so I thought. About an hour into the drive my phone rang, it was the dealership that I had just left. I answered it thinking it would just be a small question that I would refer to the Technical Operations Center (TOC) and continue on my way. That wasn't what hit me at all. Instead I received a very angry comptroller screaming at the top of her voice, "What sort of junk have you sold us?" I was dumbfounded and unable to speak while the verbal assault continued for several minutes. What could she be talking about? Had the sales department overpromised, as the network was functioning exactly as intended and documented through the **Scope of Work**. I had personally confirmed everything throughout the night; I even had a check sheet where completion checks had been attached to demonstrate proper functionality. How could it not be functioning as intended? The assistant comptroller had even signed off on the check sheet. I was confused to say the least.

SCOPE OF WORK
A legally binding and limiting component of a technical contract that specifies exactly what is to be accomplished, when, and with what standards of equipment.

I had no choice but to find out what was wrong. Everything was fantastic when I left the dealership. I slowly started asking questions, "OK so tell me what is not working for you." Initially it was that none of the PC's would power on, then it was that only the PC's in the accounting office would not power on, and finally it was that her PC would not power on. This really perplexed me, I had used her PC all night long when running my checks and it had functioned without so much as a hiccup. OK, time to start with a basic check, often it is the simplest things that cause the most trouble. The

© chompoo/Shutterstock.com

first question I asked is the light on the monitor on? She stated that it was and it was flashing orange, which her terminals had never done before. I asked her to find a letter "C" with a line coming out of it, which she promptly did (and even scolded me for thinking that she might not know what a power button looked like). I asked her to push it, she said she had been doing that but it always came back to a flashing orange button. So her monitor was on, but not her PC. I instructed her to look behind the monitor and find the other power button; she stated she had found it. I then got to listen to thirty seconds of silence. I asked what it did when she pressed it. Her first response was "oh you want me to push it?" "Yes Ma'am"—I was trying to be as polite as twenty-eight hours without sleep would let me be. Then I heard it, an absolute shriek followed by a thud. I almost drove off of the road.

The PC had come to life, her screen was flashing images and words that she had never seen before and it scared her. For the first time during the conversation, I had to physically subdue my urge to laugh out loud. I wasn't worried that I had failed on the install, I wasn't worried that equipment had failed, or that the assistant comptroller had failed in her diligence. I walked her through the logon process, and then helped her to identify her mainframe emulation icon which allowed her to get to some common ground with what she had done before.

I finished my drive home, only then did I discover that I was completely wired from the excitement of having to instruct someone in how to use the product and having been able to assist her. After the install the technical trainers were supposed to assist with teaching the skills needed to accomplish her day-to-day tasks, not realizing that she did not have the skills necessary to continue with the data long before the training would be concluded. The installer/field engineers were not supposed to be involved with that piece, but I discovered that all depends upon the client and their demands. I spent the next three weeks driving to and from the location and training the end users on the new system, at the owner's request. More importantly I developed friendships that have lasted decades, and set me on a course as a college instructor and after reflecting on this incident discovered some very important guidelines to helping others.

There are several key elements that I drew from the incident. These include have a process, understand that my education and experience is not the same for everyone (otherwise they wouldn't need me), know that a technician needs support just as much as an end user does. Even though there was a legal document, the Scope of Work (SOW) that had been drawn up, it was the process that really ensured that everything went as expected. I discovered that my experiences in Information Technology (IT) poorly prepared me for someone who did not have any experience within the modern computing environment no matter how much planning went into the process. In effect I did not really understand what was expected in this situation; neither did the customer as this represented a complete shift in paradigm for the customer and myself. I had taken for granted that the average user in the US had at least seen a personal computer if only at home. The customer had undergone extensive training in preparation for the conversion through our professional services group. It means different things to different people but it should mean that a plan has been thought through beforehand and there is a fail-safe plan of action to achieve the required results. The plan had been built over a period of several months, coordination with the appropriate teams, equipment was approved, ordered, and installed, and the conversion was executed inside of a week. As a technician I need to be flexible and patient; the customer also needed to understand that they have chosen to grow to gain more potential within their system.

COMPUTERS

So to answer the first question, what is a computer? The answer may be surprising to many people, the terminals could be considered a computer to a limited extent, as could a cell phone, and soon enough it might even include the smartphone watches. The term "computer" means something different to different people. The comptroller believed her terminal was a computer, I believed that the personal computers were "computers," we were both right. According to Merriam-Webster, computers are "programmable usually electronic device that can store, retrieve, and process data" (Computer [Def. 2, Full definition], n.d.). This definition is particularly interesting in that a computer is defined as not necessarily electronic. In the strictest sense of the word, most of us would miss the mark.

So as we move into technology, we have to understand that technology also means different things to different people. To a construction worker it could be a jackhammer; to a police officer it would include the latest in body armor that could save a life. Let's focus on Information Technology (IT). In NISTIR 7298, Revision 2, Glossary of Key Information Security

Terms, the National Institute of Science and Technology (NIST) has a very long and cumbersome definition that covers almost everything:

> Any equipment or interconnected system or subsystem of equipment that is used in the automatic acquisition, storage, manipulation, management, movement, control, display, switching, interchange, transmission, or reception of data or information by the executive agency. For purposes of the preceding sentence, equipment is used by an executive agency if the equipment is used by the executive agency directly or is used by a contractor under a contract with the executive agency which—
>
> 1.   Requires the use of such equipment; or
> 2.   Requires the use, to a significant extent, of such equipment in the performance of a service or the furnishing of a product.

The term information technology includes computers, ancillary equipment, software, firmware and similar procedures, services (including support services), and related resources.

Additionally the following line is included in 40 U.S. Code § 11101 but is not included in the NIST definition.

> "but does not include any equipment acquired by a federal contractor incidental to a federal contract."

To the comptroller, her technology was sufficient but to her general manager and franchise holder, she needed to update her technology to remain fully capable of performing her daily tasks. In essence, it is important to realize that a systems upgrade is an upgrade in workforce potential. As a business owner the cost of investment must be weighed against potential improved business operations, and most importantly a more competent workforce.

INFORMATION SECURITY

INFORMATION SECURITY
Protecting information and information systems from unauthorized access, use, disclosure, disruption, modification, or destruction.

Finally, one of the simplest but toughest questions of them all: what is **information security**? As you can tell there has already been a challenge when defining something as basic as a computer. So we have to identify what is the most important part of information security, again going to the experts in the area we turn to the law, in this case 44 U.S. Code § 3542

INTEGRITY
Guarding against improper information modification or destruction, and includes ensuring information nonrepudiation and authenticity.

CONFIDENTIALITY
Preserving authorized restrictions on access and disclosure, including means for protecting personal privacy and proprietary information.

AVAILABILITY
Ensuring timely and reliable access to and use of information.

(1) The term "information security" means protecting information and information systems from unauthorized access, use, disclosure, disruption, modification, or destruction in order to provide—

(A) **integrity**, which means guarding against improper information modification or destruction, and includes ensuring information nonrepudiation and authenticity

(B) **confidentiality**, which means preserving authorized restrictions on access and disclosure, including means for protecting personal privacy and proprietary information; and

(C) **availability**, which means ensuring timely and reliable access to and use of information.

The most important part of these elements will depend upon the organization applying the components and concepts. The organization will need to determine which of the three elements is most important; an organization that deals with legal matters might place confidentiality as the most important aspect for their business. Another organization that deals in medical information might place a greater importance on the availability and the integrity of their medical records, with only a slight emphasis being placed on the confidentiality of their client data. No organization should discard any of the three components, but rank them according to how the organization perceives its presence in its business space.

CONCLUSION

One of the major issues in dealing with cybersecurity is the lack of ability to communicate between the technician and the user/manager. As the story with the auto dealership comptroller illustrates this is not a unique phenomenon. At one point in my early usage of computers the "blue screen of death" familiar to PC users made an appearance on my computer. After hours of struggling to correct or bypass the issue, I called tech support. The technician told me to push the F7 key while restarting the computer. So, following the directions, I pushed the F and 7 keys while pressing the power button. "Blue screen of death" reappeared. He asked if I was pressing the F7 key and I said I was. I tried it again, this time pushing the power button and then pressing the F and 7 keys. Still got the "blue screen of death." The tech on the phone couldn't understand why it wasn't starting in "safe mode" and I was thinking I was going to haul the hunk of junk to the shooting range and put it out of its misery. After about five tries the tech finally asked, "Are you pushing the F7 key at the top of the keyboard?" I suddenly looked at the keyboard and realized there was a row of keys I had never considered during this highly and ever more frustrating event—the Function keys. Simultaneously the tech and I realized that we had simply been failing to communicate. I pressed the restart button, then the F7 key, and the computer booted in "safe mode." Ten minutes later the problem was fixed and the computer was good to go.

This type of issue isn't new nor will it end with ever more available and simple to use computer devices. This type of issue with the failure to have a common lexicon that is universal across languages and cultures will continue to be problematic, demanding ever more understanding by the user and the technician. It will become an even greater issue when technicians and management have to understand each other. The next issue will be when files are corrupted and need to be repaired or recovered so the data isn't lost. This is a problem not only for sustained operations of an agency or business, but also to meet legal and audit requirements for many agencies. The next chapter will address this issue in greater detail.

QUESTIONS FOR FURTHER CONSIDERATION

1. Like the comptroller in the chapter, we've all made some basic mistakes when we work with technology. Think through some of the basic errors you've made in the past. How did these make you look to others and were you treated the same as the comptroller by your IT help desk?

2. Considering the issues of Confidentiality, Integrity, and Availability, how would you prioritize these within your place of work? How are they actually prioritized by your company/agency?

3. Looking at what you use every day, what would you classify as a "computer" by Webster's definition? How many "computers" do you use/own?

REFERENCES

40 U.S. Code § 11101 (2015).
44 U.S. Code § 3542 (2015).
Merriam-Webster. Computer [Def. 2, Full definition]. (n.d.). *Merriam-Webster Online.* http://merriam-webster.com/dictionary/citation.
NISTIR. 2013. Information Technology [Full Definition]. NISTIR 7298 Revision 2, Glossary of Key Information Security Terms. http://nvlpubs.nist.gov/nistpubs/ir/2013/NIST.IR.7298r2.pdf

CHAPTER 3

LETTING SOMEONE PEEK INSIDE YOUR DRAWERS: UNDERSTANDING FILES AND THEIR ISSUES

KEY WORDS

Availability	Data	File Encryption
Confidentiality	Data Protection	Integrity

DATA
A subset of information in an electronic format that allows it to be retrieved or transmitted.

We need to look at what it is that we are trying to protect. First it is **data**, then it is information, then business intelligence that can be used to identify strengths and weaknesses for any business or agency (yours in particular). Not every piece of data will become a piece of information that will change the world, but together many pieces of data can build an overall picture that can redefine your world.

NIST defines data as "A subset of information in an electronic format that allows it to be retrieved or transmitted" (NISTIR 7298 Revision 2, Glossary of Key Information Security Terms, 2013). A more general definition might be a fact or a collection of fact. Merriam-Webster online dictionary further defines data as:

"factual information (as measurements or statistics) used as a basis for reasoning, discussion, or calculation, 2) information output by a sensing device or organ that includes both useful and irrelevant or redundant information and must be processed to be meaningful, or 3) information in numerical form that can be digitally transmitted or processed" (2016).

Data has no meaning without having a purpose, so therefore it has no real value, right? Wrong. Data is the foundation for information, so much so that the definitions are intricately tied together. Information is defined as "An instance of an information type, or any communication or representation of knowledge such as facts, data, or opinions in any medium or form, including textual, numerical, graphic, cartographic, narrative, or audiovisual." (NISTIR 7298 Revision 2, Glossary of Key Information Security Terms, 2013). We cannot have information without data, but we can have data without information.

So how can we decide what data we should draw upon to develop information? The answer comes from middle management, not necessarily upper management. In a typical business environment middle management is what actually drives the business, not upper management (sorry folks). Upper management has been taught to keep their hands off unless middle management is truly failing or a very specific use case shows up. The rest of the time middle management runs day-to-day operations. While this may bruise some egos, think about it from the corporation point of view. A "C" level officer cannot manage all of the employees within the organization, nor can a middle level manager handle all of them. We break up the organizational structure to allow small "teams" or departments to operate, these are led by middle and low level managers who in turn define many of the business requirements for the organization—much like the story book *The Richest Man in Babylon*[1]—let the experts be the experts (Clason 2007). The true strength comes from expert knowledge, and for upper management their true strength comes from letting the experts run the business.

So how does this guide the collection of data? Simply put, the experts (middle management) have decided what information they need to know—right, wrong, or indifferent. The information requirements drive existing data requirements for the organization. This information ultimately shapes the business intelligence that the organization consumes and feeds to senior leadership. In essence, middle management "manages" the perspective of senior leadership by deciding what information gets to them. That is the value of data; it can change the course of an organization with very little to no effort.

---

1. *The Richest Man in Babylon* involves a series of business lessons that are learned through a series of mishaps and missteps that cost him his fortune over and over again. It is a classic reading that is a must for anyone who wants to understand their working environment, whether at home or in the business world. The book is extremely short and is worth the read, because of the humorous presentation and the clarification of many of the pitfalls that modern people tend to fall into. One of the most important is "Illusory Superiority" which prevents us from taking advice from an expert as we believe we are more intelligent than the expert.

So how do we identify what "data" we need? We start with the intelligence that we will need to grow our business, and we do that by identifying what our business is. A clear understanding of what we do is critical for our identification of what intelligence will support our business. Data collection is fundamentally based upon answering a simple question—"Why?" Now we can work toward identifying what is required from our information, and from there, from our data. This all could go horribly wrong though.

If we misidentify what is needed then we will misidentify the information requirements and ultimately the data requirements. So what happens if we miss the mark? Simple, we will get the right information for the wrong question. Here's an example (strictly hypothetical to highlight the decision-making process): An organization has identified that it wants to sell thingy-ma-bobbers. It has identified that the thingy-ma-bobbers will do a certain task (let's say sweep up accidental environmental spills). They originally did market research and identified that out of twenty-five clients, twenty-four of them typically have an environmental spill every year. This looks pretty bleak, so everyone should be interested in this product right? Well, the senior vice president of marketing wasn't told that the survey only included twenty-four clients (and the VP assumed that his marketing department group had properly evaluated the market). The VP then orders these products into full production—preparing to see the next major product line develop. Sadly, the organization then only sells twenty-six of the thingy-ma-bobbers. After all, they were able to sell to the original twenty-four and picked up another two clients who could see the potential. The VP is terminated for spending $25 million on product development without having properly identified the market.

So what went wrong? Truthfully it was a failure on the part of the VP, but also on the folks who fed the information up the chain (middle management). While the VP was ultimately held responsible, the folks spoon-feeding information up should also be held accountable—they did form the vision of the market by choosing what data should be collected and what information would be developed, which became the business intelligence that the VP used to make a decision.

Business intelligence for one organization may not be viable as information in another organization, much less as business intelligence; it will depend again upon the goals of the organization. A sample business data cycle is shown on the following page (remember this is simplified and only a sample).

Notice directional arrows are missing. This is because the cycle is normally read clockwise, but when read counter-clockwise the cycle still makes

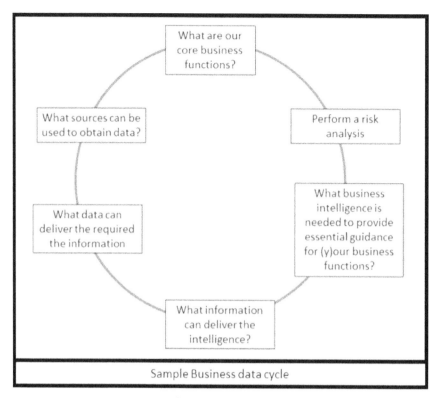

Sample Business data cycle

Source: Ervin Frenzel

sense. The essential organizational question sits at the topmost position "What are our core business functions?" This single question is the most important question that can be asked—it defines everything else within our cycle and more importantly the data we gather should reinforce our business functions. If the data does not then we are incorrectly gathering, analyzing, or interpreting it. OK, so now we have a grasp of why, we should look at the how do we handle data. More importantly we should look at how data is formatted, stored, read, and manipulated.

DATA FORMAT

Data is not visualized or even read by a computer in the same way that people visualize data. A computer is only capable of reading two states (on and off). These pieces of data are represented as "0's" and "1's" in binary language, after all a computer cannot read and interpret information in the same manner that we do. These 1's and 0's are referred to as bits.

As humans we are taught from a very early age to understand nuances of the spoken language that we hear from those around us, so our "programming" starts long before we start formalized education. A computer does not have the same programming requirement that people have. We take years to prepare for our education. A computer rolls off of the assembly line and is prepared to receive instruction immediately when it is turned on. In short, we see words; the computer cannot comprehend words and instead sees 1's and 0's. This usage requires a very simple but effective programming language; that is why binary was designed and used. The same language is used today. When data is transferred it looks very illegible to the human eye, it would read much like this "00101001001100110 . . .". This combination of bits is referred to as a bit stream.

As you can imagine an infinite string of 1's and 0's could take a very long time to write out and worse, how could you store it? The answer is simple—store it in a circle—specifically in a spiral on a circle and you can write and read for a very long time. This method of storing data has been fundamental to storing data since we first began to write to tapes years ago, then we moved to floppy disks and hard drives. It was an easy visualization and more importantly it was easy to move from our physical world to our digital world. Just like our physical world, things work best when organized—so an organization methodology had to be created and it was. The following graphic is a visualization of how data was written to tape. As time progressed this same methodology was used to write to other media (including floppy and hard discs). It is important to note that media did not start out as magnetic media. Initially we used paper tapes and punch cards to program computers, magnetic media showed up when a more durable solution was needed. Eventually you can remove the tape media from the visualization.[2] After all, why recreate a methodology every time you develop new media. The media was reusable.

---

2. Tape media needs to be replaced after a fairly short period. In the past it was shown that tapes typically started to fail after forty usages or less—so if performing a weekly backup it was good for forty weeks at fewer than one backup per week. After this it was no longer viable to assume the tapes would continue to function as backups. Modern tapes typically have improved longevity, but if your organization goes with a tape backup ensure that you investigate the continuation costs of using tape backups including how often they should be replaced. Don't let failed tapes lose your data. For that matter don't go cheap on modern hard drives either; in the past I worked for an organization that refused to let our IT department order a hard drive ($89 cost). The drive failed, costing the organization almost $150,000 in data recovery and still not everything was recovered.

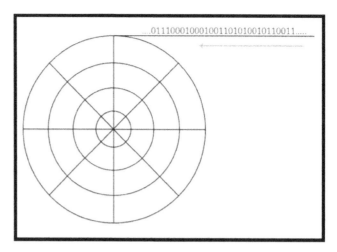

Source: Ervin Frenzel

When we moved to floppy drives and hard drives, the disks were segregated by different sectors. These were numbered and a directory was placed on the drive(s) themselves to allow easy retrieval of information (bits and bytes).

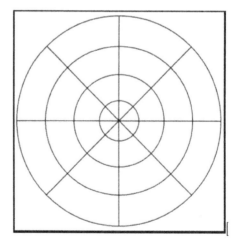

Source: Ervin Frenzel

The 1 and 0 is written by a very precise magnet, which instead of writing into eight sectors as shown above writes into a specified number of sectors according to the manufacturer. The surface of the drive is of course covered with a very precise coating of metal material which is set to receive magnetization.

DATA PROTECTION
Securing data from
unauthorized access.

DATA PROTECTION

We now know that data is stored as nothing more than a series of 1's and 0's, after all a computer does not know English, Spanish, Russian, Thai, or any other language, but it does know data is stored in binary code and that is how it reads. That is also how it knows what instructions to follow, where to route things, and how to understand everything in its environment. There is a lot of very mundane data that travels with little or no value by itself, but when combined with other data it becomes very useful information. The real question here is who will find that information useful, your organization or someone else's? So now we must protect our data.

We have to view our data as a resource, after all others already do. There are individuals, organizations, and even nation-states that view our measly data sets as very valuable. Truthfully attackers come in every shape and size, they have as many different motives as defenders have for defending data. Some reasons include because it is a job; it is something to do; the organization has committed a wrong in the eyes of the attacker; an individual has committed a wrong; or even an attacker accidentally stumbled into something that looks interesting. There is no single "one size fits all" attack, but multiple methodologies and multiple attack patterns[3] that can be used to describe how multiple types of attacks unfold. Two primary data states must be addressed; static and while in transit to properly understand data vulnerabilities.

DATA CONDITIONS

Data can be found in two different states. It can be found static (stationary) or in state of transit (in motion). The differences are like night and day.

Static Data

First, data in a static position: this is normally found in database, in a file, or on a drive of some kind (either a removable drive, or inside of a data center). This data should be encrypted to protect it from prying eyes. There should be appropriate safeguards in place to prevent normal users from browsing to data and locations where sensitive information could be disclosed. Data in a static condition is normally protected by either **file encryption** or whole disk encryption. Encrypting a single file used

FILE ENCRYPTION
Enables files to be transparently encrypted to protect confidential data from attackers with physical access to the computer.

---

3. Currently there is a program to classify common attack patterns and methodologies, this can be viewed at https://capec.mitre.org/documents/An_Introduction_to_Attack_Patterns_as_a_Software_Assurance_Knowledge_Resource.pdf. Understanding your adversary is critical to defending your network and ultimately your data.

to be considered the most efficient encryption; with advances in encryption whole disk encryption is now comparable in cost. An advantage of whole disk encryption is that the encryption is applied to everything, if an attacker obtains a hard drive they have to decrypt the entire disk to obtain any data. This is a huge plus when dealing with a lost hard drive, after all the data is protected against everything except an attacker with the keys to the encryption. A disadvantage of whole disk encryption is that the drive and the operating system have to accept the encryption so that the data can be recovered during day-to-day operations. In this regard encryption can be somewhat limiting, after all Windows encryption may not work with Apple systems and vice versa.

Now we can look at single file encryption. File encryption or single file encryption is less limiting than whole drive encryption. It also counters a large disadvantage that whole disk encryption has. If a hard drive is on and now in an unencrypted state anyone who can browse to the drive can technically see everything on the drive—unless there are file and directory restrictions to limit who can gain access to files on the system or individual files are encrypted. So the best possible condition for static data might be whole drive encryption with very important files being encrypted on the drive.

Data in Transition (In transit)

Data in motion from a single machine to a server or from machine to machine is exceptionally vulnerable. The reason is very basic, static data means an attacker must visit the device where the data is stored. We can simply guard the data set and see who reaches out to it. Data in transit is already somewhat in jeopardy. An attacker who is silently (or passively) listening simply must view the information as it passes from one device to another device on the network. Motion attracts attention. A system administrator may not even be aware that the information has been observed, or worse, copied. Once copied the information may leave the network without raising any suspicion at all, especially if no data inspection is occurring before data is sent out (this inspection is often referred to as Data Loss Prevention or DLP).

ENCRYPTION

So what is encryption? Well we can start with what it isn't. Our original data is called plain text. Plain text data is always in jeopardy, it has no protection from prying eyes or loss. To protect our plain text data we have to change its structure, once changed it becomes known as cipher text. This is when our data is no longer human readable, or for that matter it may not even be computer readable. So the process goes something like this. Plain text becomes cipher text by having encryption applied to the plain text. To go back to plain text it has to be deciphered.

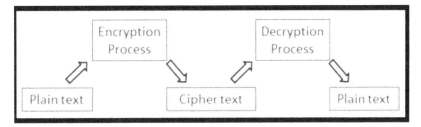

Source: Ervin Frenzel

The process needs something to work, like any lock, because encryption is a type of lock. There needs to be a key. To better understand this we need to know about the key or keys. There are two types that we should be aware of. The first is a shared key, this is like having a lock with many different copies of the key so that anyone with a copy of the key can unlock the lock. This is normally referred to as shared key encryption.

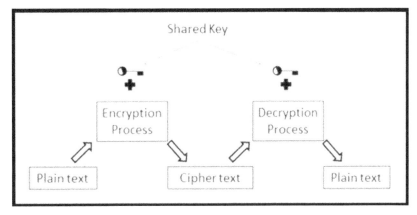

Source: Ervin Frenzel

A key weakness here is that if the key is compromised it may be some time before it is discovered as there are so many copies of it around. There is no guarantee that the person who sent the information is really who sent it. This guarantee is called non-repudiation, and in a shared key situation there is no non-repudiation (no guarantee the person sending or receiving is the person we want it to be). After all the key for both the sender and the receiver have the same key.

The other situation is referred to as public/private key encryption. It is very similar to a previous condition in that a lock is applied and a public key is used to open the lock. The key in this scenario is opposite the lock, it looks something like this:

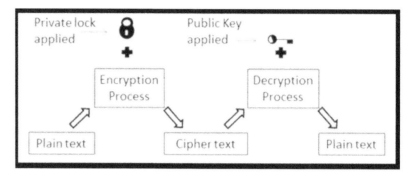

Source: Ervin Frenzel

Now for data in motion, encryption gets a little confusing at this point. After all, the key now has to be distributed without being compromised. We can do this by delivering the key through a separate channel (often called "out of band"). Using this process we can guarantee the person sending the original plain text is the person who should be sending it. This is what we typically think of as a lock and key type of mechanism, many people can see it or lock the lock but only one person can unlock the lock with their key. We can now establish non-repudiation.

NON-REPUDIATION

We have mentioned non-repudiation several times, but not really explained what it is. Remember the cipher text that we mentioned previously, well how can we be sure that it hasn't been changed? The answer is non-repudiation. There are three distinct possibilities for non-repudiation, the first is non-repudiation of the sender while the second is non-repudiation of the receiver and the final is the non-repudiation of the message itself. We have to establish (a) who is the sender and (b) who is the receiver. The person initiating the conversation will be called the sender (even though this will flip-flop throughout the conversation) for this demonstration. The sender will need to have a key known only to that individual, referred to as a "private" key—the same private key we mentioned earlier.

Sender non-repudiation is a very basic need for secure communication; it is a focus on the integrity of the message and confirmation of the sender. The message is created and converted to cipher text, then a "hash" or "message digest" is created by running an algorithm[4] against the cipher test itself. The hash/message digest might be thought of as a value that is specific to the message itself (if all messages throughout the world were to receive a unique serial number). The hash or digest is then once again encrypted (using the senders' private key) and a new value is produced, this is then considered to be a signature (or the document is considered to be "signed"). In theory and in practice the value produced will be compared to validate that the message has not been changed and that only the stated sender could have sent it.

Receiver non-repudiation will use the same type of process, except that the receiver's private key will be required to hash the receipt message. The process would change in that the sender's identity has now been verified through the sender non-repudiation process, the sender sent a message with a return receipt type of request. The message that would normally say the message has been received, at this point the roles are reversed and the receiver goes through a sender non-repudiation process of their own.

The final non-repudiation process is message non-repudiation—surprisingly we have talked about this without talking about it directly throughout the entire chapter. We simply run the hashing mechanism against the cipher text itself. The initial results will be compared with results that repeat the process at the destination. As long as both results are the same the message should be guaranteed to be the same message.

ONE FINAL WARNING

There is a point where two messages can produce the same results, this is called a collision. Care must be taken to prevent algorithms that produce collisions from being used, or at least too many collisions. No algorithm is perfect but some are weaker than others, so do some homework when researching which algorithms to use when producing hashes or message digests.

CIA TRIANGLE

So why is this important—our data cannot be compromised right? Not exactly. We need to safeguard against three separate types of compromises,

---

4. The algorithm may be a Message Digest Algorithm (MDA), a Secure Hash Algorithm (SHA), or any algorithm so designated. The algorithm is a mechanism that produces a result which cannot be reversed, leaving only a result which can be compared after having been received at the final location.

INTEGRITY
Guarding against improper information modification or destruction, and includes ensuring information nonrepudiation and authenticity.

CONFIDENTIALITY
Preserving authorized restrictions on access and disclosure, including means for protecting personal privacy and proprietary information.

AVAILABILITY
Ensuring timely and reliable access to and use of information.

these are: compromises of **integrity**, **confidentiality**, and **availability**. These three factors are called the CIA triangle.[5]

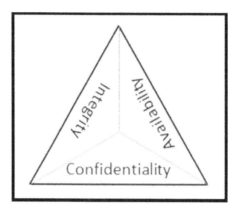

Source: Ervin Frenzel

No factor is considered more important than another, as a general rule. Each organization will need to determine the order in which to consider the factors. One company may need to protect the integrity of their data, but may not consider availability a high priority. Confidentiality deals with a basic premise; we are attempting to protect information from being disclosed to unauthorized parties (only available to those who should have access to it). Availability of course deals with making sure data is available to the appropriate people at the appropriate time. Integrity is much more complex, we have to protect the system that the data is stored in addition to protecting the data itself. We have to prevent the data from being altered either intentionally or unintentionally.

CONCLUSION

Data is valuable, your data is even more valuable not only to you but to others who may want to steal it for their own purposes. Care has to be taken that an organization doesn't carelessly give away their data with contracts to partners who wish to only gather data without providing services back to those they take data from. An organization should consider their data valuable and safeguard it as they would any other currency, especially when they create contracts or sign contracts. Safeguards may include encrypting data, whether in transit or at rest. These safeguards can use shared keys or private key infrastructure (PKI). Other measures may include non-repudiation for the sender, the receiver, or even the message itself.

---

5. The CIA triangle deals with protecting data throughout the entire data lifecycle. Its understanding is considered essential to protecting data.

QUESTIONS FOR FURTHER CONSIDERATION

1. Why might some organizations try to obtain information from clients that they might not otherwise be entitled to? What is the value of your data?

2. Which would be the most appropriate method of protecting data at your organization?

3. What is the value of non-repudiation? For the sender? The receiver? The message itself?

4. In which order would you rate confidentiality, availability, and integrity in your organization and why?

5. Would (do) you use encryption in your personal transactions? If so how would you use or how do you use it? Should you use it more frequently?

6. How can you encourage others to address encryption in their lives? And is it appropriate?

REFERENCES

Clason, G. S. 2007. The richest man in Babylon.

NISTIR 7298 Revision 2, Glossary of Key Information Security Terms. 2013. Data [Full Definition]. http://nvlpubs.nist.gov/nistpubs/ir/2013/NIST.IR.7298r2.pdf.

NISTIR 7298 Revision 2, Glossary of Key Information Security Terms. 2013. Information [Full Definition]. http://nvlpubs.nist.gov/nistpubs/ir/2013/NIST.IR.7298r2.pdf.

Merriam Webster Online Dictionary. 2016. http://www.merriam-webster.com/dictionary/data.

CHAPTER 4

CYBERCRIME: THE REASON FOR ENCRYPTION

KEY WORDS

Asset	Investment Fraud	Reshipping
Auction Fraud	Lotteries	Risk
Debt Elimination	Modification	SPAM
Fabrication	Nigerian Letter	Spoofing
Identity Theft	Phishing	Theft
Interception	Ponzi/Pyramid	Threats
Internet Extortion	Ransomware	Vulnerabilities
Interruption		

On Monday, February 15, 2016, the Moscow-based cybersecurity firm Kaspersky Lab released a report showing international hackers had stolen as much as $1 billion from one hundred banks across thirty countries through use of the *Carbanak* malware. The attack took years to accomplish, starting in 2013, and used spear phishing and other techniques to infect employee computers and then the bank networks. In some institutions the hackers had such control of the bank systems they could force remote ATMs to dispense cash to waiting thieves. Others were transfers of funds to offshore accounts in amounts ranging from $2.5 million to $10 million at a time (Virus News 2016). According to Sergey Golovanov, Principal Security Researcher at Kaspersky Lab's Global Research and Analysis Team,

> "These bank heists were surprising because it made no difference to the criminals what software the banks were using. So, even if its software is unique, a bank cannot get complacent. The attackers didn't even need to hack into the banks' services: once they got into the

network, they learned how to hide their malicious plot behind legitimate actions. It was a very slick and professional cyber-robbery." (Virus News 2016)

In 2015 the dating and affair websites, Ashley Madison and Established Men, operated by Avid Life Media (ALM) out of Toronto, was hacked by The Impact Team, a group that threatened to release ALM's user databases, source code repositories, financial records, and e-mail system. Apparently The Impact Team had problems with ALM selling customers a "Full Delete" option that would supposedly remove all traces of the customer. Unfortunately, while ALM developed a multi-million-dollar revenue stream from Full Delete, according to The Impact Team ALM didn't actually delete the financial transactions or personal information of clients. They informed ALM of this problem in July 2015 and demanded Ashley Madison and Established Men be taken down from the web. When the websites were still up and operating the following month, The Impact Team released 9.7 gigabytes of data including names, addresses, phone numbers, encrypted passwords, and credit card transaction details for about 32 million users. The information was made available on the dark web using an Onion[1] address accessible through the Tor[2] browser (Ashford 2015).

The FBI reported in late August 2015 that business e-mail compromise had risen by 270 percent between January and July 2015. Scammers were targeting businesses with e-mail that appeared to be from the corporation's CEO to direct accounting departments to transfer funds immediately (that day) to accounts or banks that the accountant would subsequently be informed of by a lawyer. A person purporting to be a lawyer would then e-mail the

---

1. Franck Dernoncourt, "What is an .onion site and why are they used?" (2016) https://www.quora.com/What-is-an-onion-site-and-why-are-they-used". onion is a pseudo-top-level domain host suffix (similar in concept to such endings as .bitnet and .uucp used in earlier times) designating an anonymous hidden service reachable via the Tor network. Such addresses are not actual DNS names, and the .onion TLD is not in the Internet DNS root, but with the appropriate proxy software installed, Internet programs such as Web browsers can access sites with .onion addresses by sending the request through the network of Tor servers. The purpose of using such a system is to make both the information provider and the person accessing the information more difficult to trace, whether by one another, by an intermediate network host, or by an outsider. Addresses in the .onion pseudo-TLD are opaque, non-mnemonic, 16-character alpha-semi-numeric hashes which are automatically generated based on a public key when a hidden service is configured. These 16-character hashes can be made up of any letter of the alphabet, and decimal digits beginning with 2 and ending with 7, thus representing an 80-bit number in base32."
2. Tor is free software for enabling anonymous communication. The name is derived from an acronym for the original software project name "The Onion Router." Tor routes traffic through a free, worldwide, volunteer network consisting of over 7,000 relays to conceal a user's location and usage from those surveilling network traffic. We discuss Tor in more detail in another chapter.

accountant with a corporate letterhead document over the CEO's signature directing the transfer of the funds to a particular bank account. From late 2013 to mid-2015, about eighteen months, over "7,000 U.S. companies had been victimized—with total dollar losses exceeding $740 million." (Stories 2015) That's exclusive of non-reported losses and victims outside of the US.

> "The scam succeeds by compromising legitimate business e-mail accounts through social engineering or computer intrusion techniques. Businesses of all sizes are targeted, and the fraud is proliferating. . . . Victim companies have come from all 50 states and nearly 80 countries. The majority of the fraudulent transfers end up in Chinese banks." (Stories 2015)

CYBERCRIME IS NOT NEW

Every year any number of cybersecurity companies release statistics of their analysis of the previous year's investigations. From January 2002 through April 2016 the Symantec Corporation has issued twenty Internet Security Threat Reports. From January 2007 through May 2011 they issued fifty-three monthly Spam Reports. McAfee Labs issues similar reports as well as predictions for the upcoming year. For most people and businesses, we simply don't have the time to read all these reports, determine if we've been subject to compromise, and understand what to do about the threats that are constantly probing for vulnerability and attacking our IT systems. We don't read the FBI crime news releases unless our local news station, paper, a magazine we routinely read, or a national story arises from the press release. Even if we are tech savvy and have news feeds and alerts coming into our tablets, pads, and smartphones—not many of us actually take the time to read and evaluate the detailed information the news feed is based upon. There is simply more information than any human has time to absorb.

Yet, there is a great deal we can learn from the summaries of reports released by our security contractors, and their competitors. For example, the 2016 Trustwave[3] Global Security Report summarized their investigations of 2015 security breaches across seventeen countries, tens of millions of vulnerability scans, tens of millions of web transactions, tens of billions of e-mail messages, and the results of thousands of penetration tests they

---

3. The authors are not endorsing any particular cybersecurity or information security company. There are any number of reports that could have been incorporated into this chapter to demonstrate the nature of the threats posed by cybercrime. We simply chose one based only on its accessibility and ease of reading the content. We could have as easily used the Symantec or McAfee cybercrime reports.

conducted across databases, networks, and applications (2016 Trustwave Global Security Report). Their findings can be summarized as:

Data Compromise

▶ 40% of investigations were of corporate and internal network breaches, and 38% were of e-commerce breaches

▶ 85% of compromised e-commerce systems used the Magento open-source platform

▶ 60% of breaches targeted payment card data

▶ 31% targeted card track (magnetic stripe) data recorded at point-of-sale (POS) terminals

▶ 29% targeted card data from e-commerce environments

▶ 41% of breaches were detected by victims themselves—this is up from 19% in 2014

▶ Median time between intrusion and detection was 15 days for internally detected breaches, compared to 168 days for breaches detected and reported by external parties

▶ For breaches requiring containment efforts after detection, the median time between detection and containment was one day for internally detected breaches, compared to twenty-eight days for externally detected breaches

E-mail Threats

▶ 54: The percentage of all inbound e-mail that was spam

▶ 34: The percentage point drop in spam advertising pharmaceutical products, from 73% of total spam in 2014 to 39% in 2015

▶ 5: The percentage of spam observed by Trustwave that included a malicious attachment or link

Malware

▶ 42% of the malware observed by Trustwave used obfuscation

▶ 33% of the malware observed by Trustwave used encryption

Application and Network Security

▶ 97% of applications tested by Trustwave had one or more security vulnerabilities

> ► 14: The median number of vulnerabilities per application discovered by managed Trustwave application scanning services

> ► The most common vulnerability types included session management vulnerabilities, information leakage vulnerabilities, and cross-site scripting vulnerabilities

> ► 10% of vulnerabilities discovered were rated critical or high risk

> ► Vulnerable SSL and TLS installations were the most common class of vulnerabilities detected by Trustwave network scanners

What these reports tell us is that no matter who we are, what type of business we operate, we are all vulnerable to attack. Our computers are being probed. So are our cell phones, laptops, pads, tablets, etc. When we travel we have to worry about the theft of our banking information when we use an ATM. We have to track our financial accounts and look for discrepancies and can't depend upon that once a month balancing of the checkbook to secure us from theft. No matter how large or small a business, cybersecurity and encryption are imperative to our survival.

THE LANGUAGE OF CYBERCRIME

Cybercrime uses terms that are common but often mixed up by the users. For ease of understanding we've included standard term definitions to align readers to the common phrases used within the cyber community. Cybercrime still deals with theft, fraud, counterfeiting, or denial of access.

THEFT
The physical removal of an object that is capable of being stolen without the consent of the owner and with the intention of depriving the owner of it permanently; the generic term for all crimes in which a person intentionally and fraudulently takes personal property of another without permission or consent and with the intent to convert it to the taker's use (including potential sale).

© AlikeYou/Shutterstock.com

Those legal terms have been established centuries ago and still apply today. Britannica defines Theft as the physical removal of an object that is capable of being stolen without the consent of the owner and with the intention of depriving the owner of it permanently. If the theft is of information, and that information still resides on the company servers, it has neither been physically removed nor is the owner permanently deprived of the item. Thus, is cyber theft still a crime? That depends on the dictionary and definition. According to Law.com, **Theft** is the generic term for all crimes in which a person intentionally and fraudulently takes personal property of another without permission or consent and with the intent to convert it to the taker's use (including potential sale). This definition is much more appropriate to our discussion of cybercrime as it applies directly to the issue, regardless of whether somebody took your car or took your computer files. Why the difference is important is because we need to be clear in how we define terms if we are going to be talking about crimes in cyberspace.

So, why the term cybercrime? Well, it turns out that while the fundamentals of crime haven't really changed, we still need to create terms that directly address the particular crime that has been attempted/completed. Thus, cybercrime is the "criminal activity (such as fraud, identity theft, or distribution of child pornography) committed electronically using a computer especially to illegally access, alter, or manipulate data." (Merriam-Webster.com)

INTERCEPTION
an attack on data in transit.

INTERRUPTION
an attack on availability such as a denial of service attack (or DOS). An interruption attack's aim is to make resources unavailable. Not too long ago, Wordpress.com, a popular Blog Hosting Site was faced with a DOS attack taking down the servers so the service was unavailable to its users.

MODIFICATION
an attack that tampers with a resource. Its aim is to modify information that is being communicated with two or more parties. An example of a modification attack could be sending information that was meant to go to one party but directing it to another.

FABRICATION
also known as counterfeiting. It bypasses authenticity checks, and essentially is mimicking or impersonating information. This sort of attack usually inserts new information, or records extra information on a file. It is mainly used to gain access to data or a service.

No matter what the current name may be for a particular type of cybercrime activity, the types of crime and the associated targets are always the same. Somebody is intercepting, interrupting, modifying, or outright fabricating information. Whether the technique uses phishing, malware, hacking, man-in-the-middle, ransomware, or some other means, the target and type of activity is always the same. Thus, there is little need for new legal terms to address the type of crime as the crime type is still fundamentally unchanged. Only the manner in which it is carried out has changed; and that is the reason for new terms to address cybercrime.

Similarly, the target of the crime has changed, but the effects on that target haven't changed. Except for the intentional physical destruction of infrastructure through the use of cyber systems, all other cybercrime is

RANSOMWARE
Malicious software inadvertently downloaded to a computer that subsequently locks the computer screen until an acceptable pass code is entered, usually after some sort of money transfer.

fundamentally software. Either the software (data, files, code) is being taken by somebody for a use not intended by its creator/owner, or the software is being counterfeited or corrupted to produce an outcome that results in the denial of a creator/owner to what is rightfully theirs. In the first case—files, passwords, software is taken by another. In the second case—**ransomware**, malicious code, false information is placed into an existing system to deprive the system creator/owner of their ability to access the information it contains without some expense—either payment to the malicious actor or the replacement of the system and its associated software. Payment is always made electronically. Thus, nothing ever actually changes hands. Only bytes of data are passed back and forth to the benefit of the criminal and detriment of the target.

ASSET
People, property, and information. People may include employees and customers along with other invited persons such as contractors or guests. Property assets consist of both tangible and intangible items that can be assigned a value. Intangible assets include reputation and proprietary information. Information may include databases, software code, critical company records, and many other intangible items.

THREATS
Anything that can exploit a vulnerability, intentionally or accidentally, and obtain, damage, or destroy an asset.

VULNERABILITIES
Weaknesses or gaps in a security program that can be exploited by threats to gain unauthorized access to an asset or assets.

RISK
The potential for loss, damage, or destruction of an asset as a result of a threat exploiting a vulnerability.

COUNTERING CYBERCRIME

With all this new means of stealing from others, or destroying somebody's data, we have to develop means of protecting our data and the hardware in which the data is incorporated. We lock our physical belongings behind doors that require keys or passcodes. We place extreme valuables, from jewelry and bullion to birth and marriage certificates, in locked safes where they cannot be touched by outsider's hands, fires, floods, or other hazards. So what do we do to protect electronic data that moves through the air, along fiber optic lines, and are stored in the cloud?

Fundamentally, we use the same methods of protection to secure our cyber data as we use to protect our physical belongings and important documents. We lock the data behind doors, or inside safes, with different levels of security as we feel appropriate. This is where we move into the realm of encryption, passwords, access, and authentication. We discuss these topics in more detail in subsequent chapters.

TYPES OF CYBERCRIME

With the constant changes and rapid adaption to counter crime methods, the types of cybercrime are constantly evolving, with the attackers always coming up with a new and unique method to take what is yours and put it to use for themselves. As you can see from the following list (FBI Internet Crime Complaint Center 2016), there are any numbers of ways people will attempt to steal from you.

Auction Fraud

AUCTION FRAUD
Fraud attributable to the misrepresentation of a product advertised for sale through an Internet auction site or the non-delivery of products purchased through an Internet auction site.

Auction fraud involves fraud attributable to the misrepresentation of a product advertised for sale through an Internet auction site or the non-delivery of products purchased through an Internet auction site. Consumers are strongly cautioned against entering into Internet transactions with subjects exhibiting the following behavior:

▶ The seller posts the auction as if he resides in the United States, then responds to victims with a congratulatory e-mail stating he is outside the United States for business reasons, family emergency, etc. Similarly, beware of sellers who post the auction under one name, and ask for the funds to be transferred to another individual.

▶ The subject requests funds to be wired directly to him/her via Western Union, MoneyGram, or bank-to-bank wire transfer. By using these services, the money is virtually unrecoverable with no recourse for the victim.

▶ Sellers acting as authorized dealers or factory representatives in countries where there would be no such dealers should be avoided.

▶ Buyers who ask for the purchase to be shipped using a certain method to avoid customs or taxes inside another country should be avoided.

▶ Be suspect of any credit card purchases where the address of the card holder does not match the shipping address. Always receive the card holder's authorization before shipping any products.

Auction Fraud—Romania

Auction fraud is the most prevalent of Internet crimes associated with Romania. The subjects have saturated the Internet auctions and offer almost every in-demand product. The subjects have also become more flexible, allowing victims to send half the funds now, and the other half when the item arrives. The auctions are often posted as if the seller is a United States citizen, then the subject advises the victim to send the money to a business partner, associate, sick relative, a family member, etc., usually in a European country. The money is usually transferred via MoneyGram or Western Union wire transfer. The Internet Crime Complaint Center has verified in order to receive funds via Western Union, the receiver must provide the complete information of the sender and the receiver's full name and address. The funds can be picked up anywhere in the world using this information. There is no need to provide the money transfer control number (MTCN) or the answer to any secret question, as many subjects have purported to the victims. Money sent via wire transfer leaves little recourse for the victim. The most recent trend is a large increase in bank-to-bank wire transfers. Most significantly, these wire transfers go through large United States banks and are then routed to Bucharest, Romania or Riga, Latvia. Similarly, the sellers also occasionally direct the victims to pay using phony escrow services. Sometimes actual escrow websites are compromised and other sites resembling them are created by the subjects. Once the funds are wire transferred to the escrow website, the seller discontinues contact.

Counterfeit Cashier's Check

The counterfeit cashier's check scheme targets individuals that use Internet classified advertisements to sell merchandise. Typically, an interested party located outside the United States contacts a seller. The seller is told that the buyer has an associate in the United States that owes him money. As such, he will have the associate send the seller a cashier's check for the amount owed to the buyer. The amount of the cashier's check will be thousands of dollars more than the price of the merchandise and the seller is told the excess amount will be used to pay the shipping costs associated with getting the merchandise to his location. The seller is instructed to deposit the check, and as soon as it clears, to wire the excess funds back to the buyer or to another associate identified as a shipping agent. In most instances, the money is sent to locations in West Africa (Nigeria). Because a cashier's check is used, a bank will typically release the funds immediately, or after a one- or two-day hold. Falsely believing the check has cleared, the seller wires the money as instructed. In some cases, the buyer is able to convince the seller that some circumstance has arisen that necessitates the cancellation of the sale, and is successful in conning the victim into sending the remainder of the money. Shortly thereafter, the victim's bank notifies him that the check was fraudulent, and the bank is holding the victim responsible for the full amount of the check.

Credit Card Fraud

The Internet Crime Complaint Center has received multiple reports alleging foreign subjects are using fraudulent credit cards. The unauthorized use of a credit/debit card, or card number, to fraudulently obtain money or property is considered credit card fraud. Credit/debit card numbers can be stolen from unsecured websites, or can be obtained in an **identity theft** scheme.

Debt Elimination

IDENTITY THEFT
When someone appropriates another's personal information without their knowledge to commit theft or fraud.

DEBT ELIMINATION
Generally involve websites advertising a legal way to dispose of mortgage loans and credit card debts.

Debt elimination schemes generally involve websites advertising a legal way to dispose of mortgage loans and credit card debts. Most often, all that is required of the participant is to send $1,500 to $2,000 to the subject, along with all the particulars of the participant's loan information and a special power of attorney authorizing the subject to enter into transactions regarding the title of the participant's homes on their behalf. The subject then issues bonds and promissory notes to the lenders that purport to legally satisfy the debts of the participant. In exchange, the participant is then required to pay a certain percentage of the value of the satisfied debts to the subject. The potential risk of identity theft related crimes associated with the debt elimination scheme is extremely high because the participants provide all of their personal information to the subject.

Parcel Courier E-mail Scheme

The Parcel Courier E-mail Scheme involves the supposed use of various National and International level parcel providers such as DHL, UPS, FedEx, and the USPS. Often, the victim is directly e-mailed by the subject(s) following online bidding on auction sites. Most of the scams follow a general pattern which includes the following elements:

▶ The subject instructs the buyer to provide shipping information such as name and address.

▶ The subject informs the buyer that the item will be available at the selected parcel provider in the buyer's name and address, thereby, identifying the intended receiver.

▶ The selected parcel provider checks the item and purchase documents to guarantee everything is in order.

▶ The selected parcel provider sends the buyer delivery notification verifying their receipt of the item.

▶ The buyer is instructed by the subject to go to an electronic funds transfer medium, such as Western Union, and make a funds transfer in the subject's name and in the amount of the purchase price.

▶ After the funds transfer, the buyer is instructed by the subject to forward the selected parcel provider the funds transfer identification number, as well as their name and address associated with the transaction.

▶ The subject informs the buyer the parcel provider will verify payment information and complete the delivery process.

▶ Upon completion of delivery and inspection of the item(s) by the receiver, the buyer provides the parcel provider funds transfer information, thus, allowing the seller to receive his funds.

Employment/Business Opportunities

Employment/business opportunity schemes have surfaced wherein bogus foreign-based companies are recruiting citizens in the United States on several employment-search websites for work-at-home employment opportunities. These positions often involve reselling or reshipping merchandise to destinations outside the United States. Prospective employees are required to provide personal information, as well as copies of their identification, such as a driver's license, birth certificate, or social security card. Those employees that are "hired" by these companies are then told that their salary will be paid by check from a United States company reported to be a creditor of the employer. This is done under the pretense that the employer does not have any banking set up in the United States. The amount of the check is significantly more than the employee is owed for salary and expenses, and the employee is instructed to deposit the check into their own account, and then wire the overpayment back to the employer's bank, usually located in Eastern Europe. The checks are later found to be fraudulent, often after the wire transfer has taken place.

© Maxx-Studio/Shutterstock.com

In a similar scam, some web-based international companies are advertising for affiliate opportunities, offering individuals the chance to sell high-end electronic items, such as plasma television sets and home theater systems, at significantly reduced prices. The affiliates are instructed to offer the merchandise on well-known Internet auction sites. The affiliates will accept the payments, and pay the company, typically by means of wire transfer. The company is then supposed to drop-ship the merchandise directly to the buyer, thus eliminating the need for the affiliate to stock or warehouse merchandise. The merchandise never ships, which often prompts the buyers to take legal action against the affiliates, who in essence are victims themselves.

Escrow Services Fraud

In an effort to persuade a wary Internet auction participant, the perpetrator will propose the use of a third-party escrow service to facilitate the exchange of money and merchandise. The victim is unaware the perpetrator has actually compromised a true escrow site and, in actuality, created one that closely resembles a legitimate escrow service. The victim sends payment to the phony escrow and receives nothing in return. Or, the victim sends merchandise to the subject and waits for his/her payment through the escrow site which is never received because it is not a legitimate service.

Identity Theft

Identity theft occurs when someone appropriates another's personal information without their knowledge to commit theft or fraud. Identity theft is a vehicle for perpetrating other types of fraud schemes. Typically, the victim is led to believe they are divulging sensitive personal information to a legitimate business, sometimes as a response to an e-mail solicitation to update billing or membership information, or as an application to a fraudulent Internet job posting.

Internet Extortion

Internet extortion involves hacking into and controlling various industry databases, promising to release control back to the company if funds are received, or the subjects are given web administrator jobs. Similarly, the subject will threaten to compromise information about consumers in the industry database unless funds are received.

Investment Fraud

Investment fraud is an offer using false or fraudulent claims to solicit investments or loans, or providing for the purchase, use, or trade of forged or counterfeit securities.

Lotteries

The **lottery** scheme deals with persons randomly contacting e-mail addresses advising them they have been selected as the winner of an

INTERNET EXTORTION
Hacking into and controlling various industry databases, promising to release control back to the company if funds are received, or the subjects are given web administrator jobs.

INVESTMENT FRAUD
An offer using false or fraudulent claims to solicit investments or loans, or providing for the purchase, use, or trade of forged or counterfeit securities.

LOTTERIES
Randomly contacting e-mail addresses advising them they have been selected as the winner of an international lottery.

international lottery. The Internet Crime Complaint Center has identified numerous lottery names being used in this scheme. The e-mail message usually reads similar to the following:

> This is to inform you of the release of money winnings to you. Your e-mail was randomly selected as the winner and therefore you have been approved for a lump sum payout of $500,000.00. To begin your lottery claim, please contact the processing company selected to process your winnings.

An agency name follows this body of text with a point of contact, phone number, fax number, and an e-mail address. An initial fee ranging from $1,000 to $5,000 is often requested to initiate the process and additional fee requests follow after the process has begun. These e-mails may also list a United States point of contact and address while also indicating the point of contact at a foreign address.

Nigerian Letter or "419"

NIGERIAN LETTER
The scam combines the threat of impersonation fraud with a variation of an advance fee scheme in which a letter, e-mail, or fax is received by the potential victim.

Nigerian Letter or "419" was named for the violation of Section 419 of the Nigerian Criminal Code, the 419 scam combines the threat of impersonation fraud with a variation of an advance fee scheme in which a letter, e-mail, or fax is received by the potential victim. The communication from individuals representing themselves as Nigerian or foreign government officials offers the recipient the "opportunity" to share in a percentage of millions of dollars, soliciting for help in placing large sums of money in overseas bank accounts. Payment of taxes, bribes to government officials, and legal fees are often described in great detail with the promise that all expenses will be reimbursed as soon as the funds are out of the country. The recipient is encouraged to send information to the author, such as blank letterhead stationery, bank name and account numbers, and other identifying information using a facsimile number provided in the letter. The scheme relies on convincing a willing victim to send money to the author of the letter in several installments of increasing amounts for a variety of reasons.

Phishing/Spoofing

PHISHING
Forged or faked electronic documents intended to acquire personal information to commit another Internet crime.

SPOOFING
The dissemination of e-mail which is forged to appear as though it was sent by someone other than the actual source.

Phishing and **spoofing** are somewhat synonymous in that they refer to forged or faked electronic documents. Spoofing generally refers to the dissemination of e-mail which is forged to appear as though it was sent by someone other than the actual source. Phishing, often utilized in conjunction with a spoofed e-mail, is the act of sending an e-mail falsely claiming to be an established legitimate business in an attempt to dupe the unsuspecting recipient into divulging personal, sensitive information such as passwords, credit card numbers, and bank account information after directing the user to visit a specified website. The website, however, is not genuine and was set up only as an attempt to steal the user's information.

Ponzi/Pyramid

Ponzi or pyramid schemes are investment scams in which investors are promised abnormally high profits on their investments. No investment is actually made. Early investors are paid returns with the investment money received from the later investors. The system usually collapses. The later investors do not receive dividends and lose their initial investment.

Reshipping

The "**reshipping**" scheme requires individuals in the United States, who sometimes are co-conspirators and other times are unwitting accomplices, to receive packages at their residence and subsequently repackage the merchandise for shipment, usually abroad. "Reshippers" are being recruited in various ways but the most prevalent are through employment offers and conversing, and later befriending, unsuspecting victims through Internet Relay Chat Rooms. Unknown subjects post help-wanted advertisements at popular Internet job search sites and respondents quickly reply to the online advertisement. As part of the application process, the prospective employee is required to complete an employment application, wherein he/she divulges sensitive personal information, such as their date of birth and social security number which, unbeknownst to the victim employee, will be used to obtain credit in his/her name.

The applicant is informed he/she has been hired and will be responsible for forwarding, or "reshipping" merchandise purchased in the United States to the company's overseas home office. The packages quickly begin to arrive and, as instructed, the employee dutifully forwards the packages to their overseas destination. Unbeknownst to the "reshipper," the recently received merchandise was purchased with fraudulent credit cards.

The second means of recruitment involves the victim conversing with the unknown individual in various Internet Relay Chat Rooms. After establishing this new online "friendship" or "love" relationship, the unknown subject explains for various legal reasons his/her country will not allow direct business shipments into his/her country from the United States. He/she then asks for permission to send recently purchased items to the victim's United States address for subsequent shipment abroad for which the unknown subject explains he/she will cover all shipping expenses.

After the United States citizen agrees, the packages start to arrive at great speed. This fraudulent scheme lasts several weeks until the "reshipper" is contacted. The victimized merchants explain to the "reshipper" the recent shipments were purchased with fraudulent credit cards. Shortly thereafter, the strings of attachment are untangled and the boyfriend/girlfriend realizes their cyber relationship was nothing more than an Internet scam to help facilitate the transfer of goods purchased online by fraudulent means.

SPAM

SPAM
Unsolicited bulk e-mail.

With improved technology and worldwide Internet access, **spam**, or unsolicited bulk e-mail, is now a widely used medium for committing traditional white collar crimes including financial institution fraud, credit card fraud, and identity theft, among others. It is usually considered unsolicited because the recipients have not opted to receive the e-mail. Generally, this bulk e-mail refers to multiple identical messages sent simultaneously. Those sending this spam are violating the Controlling the Assault of Non-Solicited Pornography and Marketing (CAN-SPAM) Act, Title 18, U.S. Code, Section 1037. Spam can also act as the vehicle for accessing computers and servers without authorization and transmitting viruses and botnets. The subjects masterminding this spam often provide hosting services and sell open proxy information, credit card information, and e-mail lists illegally.

© Feng Yu/Shutterstock.com

Third Party Receiver of Funds

A general trend has been noted by the Internet Crime Complaint Center regarding work-at-home schemes on websites. In several instances, the subjects, usually foreign, post work-at-home job offers on popular Internet employment sites, soliciting for assistance from United States citizens. The subjects allegedly are posting Internet auctions, but cannot receive the proceeds from these auctions directly because his/her location outside the United States makes receiving these funds difficult. The seller asks the United States citizen to act as a third party receiver of funds from victims who have purchased products from the subject via the Internet. The United States citizen, receiving the funds from the victims, then wires the money to the subject.

CONCLUSION

Keith Poyser, general manager for Europe at security firm Accellion, said in an interview with ComputerWeekly.com that the lesson to be learnt from the Ashley Madison data breech is that no business can afford to take cybersecurity and data protection lightly. "We have seen breach after breach in the last two years, from Carphone Warehouse to Target and Sony, to name a few," he said. "This is a cyber arms race with criminal techniques constantly evolving, which means defence [sic] . . . must also evolve. . . ." (Ashford 2015). Prevention makes more sense. This requires major investment in security at all layers of the process. Poyser goes on to say that business culture must evolve, it must incorporate cybersecurity at all levels. While many businesses have solid network defenses, asset layer management and protection, and personnel education on security, many more still use non-secured, public cloud services or leave their content with inadequate protection. Therefore, the sophistication of cyber criminals will increase and web users will never feel completely safe. It is the responsibility of the gatekeepers to do everything possible to keep data secure and for management to enable those gatekeepers to do their jobs.

QUESTIONS FOR FURTHER CONSIDERATION

1. The Internet has created a whole new way for traditional criminal activities to expand their reach. Where do you see the next criminal effort to go?

2. What types of gatekeeper protection do you maintain on your computers? Do they work? How can you tell?

3. We all use more than just our computers. In addition to our computers, what other computer devices do you use every day? This is a trick question—instead of thinking specifically about computers—think about everyplace there is a computer chip (integrated circuit) with the ability to access communications technology.

REFERENCES

2016 Trustwave Global Security Report, p. 7. https://www2.trustwave.com/rs/815-RFM-693/images/2016%20Trustwave%20Global%20Security%20Report.pdf.

Ashford, Warwick. 2015. ComputerWeekly.com. Ashley Madison hackers carry out threat to publish user data (August 19). http://www.computerweekly.com/news/4500251966/Ashley-Madison-hackers-carry-out-threat-to-publish-user-data.

FBI Internet Crime Complaint Center (IC3). 2016. https://www.ic3.gov/crimeschemes.aspx.

Merriam-Webster.com. "cybercrime." http://www.merriam-webster.com/dictionary/cybercrime.

Stories. 2015. "Business E-Mail Compromise: an emerging global threat" (August 28). FBI.gov. https://www.fbi.gov/news/stories/2015/august/business-e-mail-compromise/business-e-mail-compromise.

Virus News. 2016. "The Great Bank Robbery: Carbanak cybergang steals $1bn from 100 financial institutions worldwide." Kaspersky lab. http://www.kaspersky.com/about/news/virus/2015/Carbanak-cybergang-steals-1-bn-USD-from-100-financial-institutions-worldwide.

CHAPTER 5

INTRODUCTION TO ENCRYPTION

KEY WORDS

Asymmetric Encryption	Data Block Encryption	Public Key
Bit Stream	Hashing	Public Key Infrastructure (PKI)
Block Cipher	Non-Repudiation	Salting
Cipher block chaining	On the Fly	Shared Key
Cipher Text	Plain Text	Streaming Encryption
Data at Rest	Private Key	Symmetric Encryption

ABCD**EF**G**H**IJK**L**MNO PQRSTUVWXYZ

DEFG**H**IJKLMNOPQRSTUVWXYZABC

transforms "HELLO" to "KHOOR"

"A simple Caesar Cipher"

INTRODUCTION TO ENCRYPTION

ENCRYPTION
When data is altered from its original form by use of cipher text: the process of changing plain text into cipher text for the purpose of security or privacy.

Encryption is neither new nor unique. Over 2,000 years ago Julius Caesar created a cipher system to encode and decode orders to his field commanders. This simple character shift device was basic encryption and has become the basis of all encryption up to the present. The next step in cipher development was a random substitution of characters for other characters, requiring a more specific key to break. These can get quite complex, particularly when replacing letters with symbols, but they are still fundamentally shift ciphers, just using a variety of character sources. While there are some encryption systems that go far beyond character substitution, they tend to be very limited in applicability and usability by the general public. However, shift and substitution ciphers are still in use today and still function quite well, particularly when the cipher uses multi-layered keys.

COMPUTERS AND ENCRYPTION

So, let's talk about protecting data. Computer data is neither magic nor mythical, it is simply bits and bytes. What this means is that data is a physical thing that can be controlled. As a manager, you have a primary responsibility to the organization to ensure that this physical thing doesn't leave your protection without authorization. Data is pretty much like any other resource that you must protect for your organization. Remember resources are what make your organization successful. The only difference is that you cannot see the bits and bytes without a computer, but then again neither can others. They can see your data just as easily as you can, but what if you do not want them to see it? The answer is simple; people believe you can either hide your data or protect it. These two concepts can be implemented in many different ways that you as a manager and your technicians implementing security need to stay in fairly common communication, just so you know how the organizational security implementation is occurring.

© Rawpixel.com/Shutterstock.com

In combat there are really two factors to be considered when coming under fire—cover and concealment. An example of concealment would be very simple; as you are walking down the street an attacker starts shooting at you. You hide behind a bush so that the person shooting has a lesser chance of seeing you and therefore a smaller chance of successfully shooting you. Cover on the other hand means that as you walk down the street and an attacker starts shooting at you, you can now hide behind a boulder or hide in an area where the enemy cannot hit you while shooting directly at you. This doesn't mean that the attacker cannot hit you if the attacker fires indirectly or from a different vantage point. The main point is that concealment hides your data from view (it is still there and if someone looks hard enough they will see it). This is basically what you do when you obfuscate data or even when you mask it. Cover protects data from direct observation (and prevents someone from directly engaging it); this is common when a database is contained on a separate server or certain data is kept offline for its protection.

Face it, data has to be connected for it to be useful. As a general rule, a dedicated attacker will find the hidden data. In the age of digital information very little can be hidden. In fact data cannot really be hidden no matter how hard you try. An old security axiom: there is no security by obscurity. If data is somehow connected to a network, it will be exposed so that someone can see it. Whether that someone is you, someone you allow to see your data, or someone you do not want to see it doesn't matter. While you may believe that you can successfully hide your data, there is always someone who is better at seeking than you could ever be at hiding.

Now that we know that we cannot simply hide our data, let's look at actually protecting it. The act of providing cover is fairly straightforward. We can disconnect it from the network, in which case it provides less value for us or we can lock it in containers so that it can be used and provide the value that we need.

There are two times that encryption should be applied. The first is when we store data, referred to as "**data at rest**" this is the point at which nothing is accessing the data so it is simply being stored. The second time to encrypt data is when it is in motion, often referred to as "**on the fly**." Data in motion is at a higher risk than data at rest due to sniffing or passive observation, because it is passing through multiple devices. Data at rest is at a greater risk of being stolen by an active attacker, as larger concentrations of data are now grouped together. Both data states have their own individual strengths and weaknesses.

This is the point where we address encryption. We physically place a lock on our bits and bytes. We are not simply hiding them as we could with concealment, but physically lock them up to protect them from those who want them exposed for their own gain. In essence, we are changing data so that it is no longer hidden but is in its own little world, in which only a certain key will allow it to be directly viewed.

We typically use two types of encryption, **symmetric** and **asymmetric**. Don't let the terms confuse you, they simply mean that the key used to encrypt is either the same or different from the key used to decrypt the information. Symmetric encryption will use the same key while asymmetric will use a different key for the decryption.

So, what is encryption? NIST states that encryption is "The process of changing **plain text** into **cipher text** for the purpose of security or privacy" (NISTIR 7298 Revision 2, 2013). Given this we must first define "what is

DATA AT REST
Data is being stored.

ON THE FLY
Data in motion.

SYMMETRIC ENCRYPTION
A form of computerized cryptography using a singular encryption key to guise an electronic message.

ASYMMETRIC ENCRYPTION
A form of encryption where keys come in pairs. . . . Frequently (but not necessarily), the keys are interchangeable, in the sense that if key A encrypts a message, then B can decrypt it, and if key B encrypts a message, then key A can decrypt it.

PLAIN TEXT
Data as we would normally read it.

CIPHER TEXT
The plain text that has been changed, so that it is not easily distinguishable for people, to prevent unauthorized disclosure (providing us either security or privacy).

plain text?" and "what is cipher text?" These are easy to define. Plain text is exactly that, data as we would normally read it. Cipher text is the plain text that has been changed, so that it is not easily distinguishable for people, to prevent unauthorized disclosure (providing us either security or privacy). The encryption process will need a key, just like any other lock, or the lock will become so effective that we cannot unlock our own information. This is typically called a "**private key**" but this term can become very confusing as we will discuss shortly. The encryption process now looks like this:

PRIVATE KEY
A shared algorithm between all members of the same group; one key in a two-key pair.

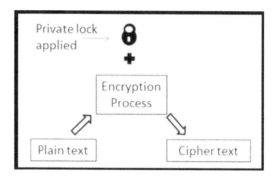

Source: Ervin Frenzel

SHARED KEY
A shared algorithm between all members of the same group.

NON-REPUDIATION
Ability to determine who performs an action; assurance that the sender of information is provided with proof of delivery and the recipient is provided with proof of the sender's identity, so neither can later deny having processed the information.

PUBLIC KEY
The second key in a two-key pair.

PUBLIC KEY INFRASTRUCTURE (PKI)
System used for sending and receiving information without exposing it to unauthorized individuals.

Now for a brief explanation of private key: in the symmetric world, this key is a shared algorithm between all members of the same group. This is sometimes called a "**shared key**." So, this would be equivalent to having a house with a large number of copies of the door key, the home owner needs to be careful of who gets a copy as the owner cannot guarantee that the recipient will not make additional copies, loan a key to someone else, or even misplace or destroy the key. While this system controls access to the data we could never determine who locked or who unlocked a given document, this ability to determine who performs an action is called "**non-repudiation**." In the asymmetric world, the term "private key" refers to one key in a two-key pair—the first key is known as a private key while the second key is known as a **public key**. The two keys work together; the private key is used to encrypt the message and send to a large quantity of people. This is the basis for the **Public Key Infrastructure (PKI)** system used for sending and receiving information without exposing it to unauthorized individuals. Anyone with the public key could then decrypt the message and read it. This allows the message to be sent to many people. If someone replies to this message with the public key, only the person who possesses the private key can now decrypt the message. This, however, prevents the recipient from being able to guarantee who actually sent the message. In either case the transaction now looks something like this:

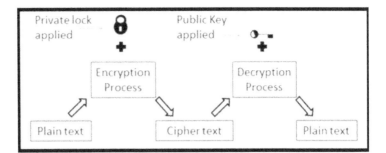

Source: Ervin Frenzel

HASHING OVERVIEW

A key element here is the concept of encryption versus the **hashing** process. Encryption is a two-way process meaning that everything that is done is meant to be undone at some point in the future. When we want to verify the value of a file or given pieces of data we hash the original data. The process is very simple. The data is sent through an algorithm, but unlike encryption, this algorithm produces a result which cannot be reversed. The final value produces a value that can be thought of much like a checksum (a value that represents the data in the original data packet). Comparing hash values from an original document versus a received document can provide an indication as to whether a document has been altered from its original state. This process will look like this:

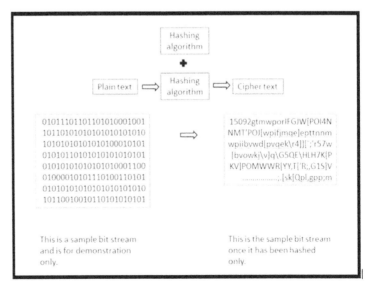

Source: Ervin Frenzel

This process will be completed again after the encryption process has been undone. The post decryption hashing algorithm results will then be compared to the pre-encryption hashing results. Two possible results are revealed, the first is that the results of the hash are exactly the same indicating that the two files are also exactly the same; the second is that the two results vary by even a single variable. This, of course, indicates that the two files are not the same (no matter how close they appear). This process, when added to the encryption process, provides for non-repudiation. NIST states that non-repudiation is:

> Assurance that the sender of information is provided with proof of delivery and the recipient is provided with proof of the sender's identity, so neither can later deny having processed the information.

> Protection against an individual falsely denying having performed a particular action. Provides the capability to determine whether a given individual took a particular action such as creating information, sending a message, approving information, and receiving a message.

> Is the security service by which the entities involved in a communication cannot deny having participated. Specifically, the sending entity cannot deny having sent a message (non-repudiation with proof of origin), and the receiving entity cannot deny having received a message (non-repudiation with proof of delivery).

> A service that is used to provide assurance of the integrity and origin of data in such a way that the integrity and origin can be verified and validated by a third party as having originated from a specific entity in possession of the private key (i.e., the signatory). (NISTIR 7298 Revision 2, Glossary of Key Information Security Terms, 2013).

There is a lot of information contained in the definitions listed above. What it amounts to is that non-repudiation can be used to verify data itself, verify the sender is really who sent it, and verify the recipient received it. This however does not encrypt the data so that it can be returned to plain text later.

STREAMING ENCRYPTION OVERVIEW

STREAMING ENCRYPTION
Takes the "bit stream" and continuously encrypts data as it is prepared to be sent.

BIT STREAM
Predetermined sized stream of data.

Now that we understand the two different locking methods, we should look at the two primary encryption processes used to encrypt the data. The first encryption technique is "**streaming**" **encryption.** This process takes the "**bit stream**" and continuously encrypts data as it is prepared to be sent. This methodology works best with data that needs to be processed quickly, such as voice or even streaming video or music. One of the most commonly used today is the RC4 (Rivest Cipher 4) cipher. Bit stream in equals cipher stream out. It looks something like this:

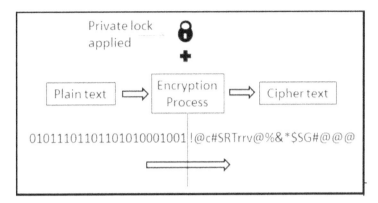

Source: Ervin Frenzel

CIPHER BLOCK AND CIPHER BLOCK CHAINING VARIATIONS

In streaming encryption techniques, we simply feed a steady stream of bits into the encryption process; this isn't always the strongest method of securing data. There are only so many ways to permeate a 1 or a 0 as it passes through an algorithm. To increase the difficulty of exposing the concealed data, it makes more sense to increase the amount of data that is encrypted at a single pass. As is expected more effort to encrypt data means that it will slow down the process and eventually the computer doing the encryption. So, this is how it works. A predetermined sized stream of data is selected (typically around 64 bits). This becomes known as a "**block**" (in some implementations additional bits are added to create a "**salting**" to start the encryption process). When this **data block** is run through the encryption process, a "round" is completed. A larger number of bits are in this individual block; therefore, this block becomes much more difficult to attack than the original stream cipher but much slower to encrypt.

BLOCK CIPHER
A method of encrypting text (to produce cipher text) in which a cryptographic key and algorithm are applied to a block of data (for example, sixty-four contiguous bits) at once as a group rather than to one bit at a time.

SALTING
Random data that is used as an additional input to a one-way function that "hashes" a password or passphrase.

DATA BLOCK
The smallest unit of data used by a database.

CIPHER BLOCK CHAINING
Mode of operation for a block cipher (one in which a sequence of bits are encrypted as a single unit or block with a cipher key applied to the entire block).

If it then goes through the process again, completing another "round" it now becomes known as **cipher block chaining**. This means that the process repeats until a given number of rounds have been completed. The implementation often dictates the number of rounds that must be completed before the cipher text is ready to send out. Once the given number of rounds is completed, the block is now encrypted and ready to ship out. Any additional data will repeat this process in the designated block size until all the data has been prepared and shipped. As you can imagine, this alone takes a considerable amount of time, which means this should only be done when heavier layers of encryption are required. In this case the block encryption will look like this:

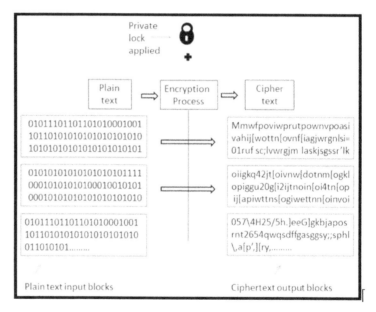

Source: Ervin Frenzel

When this becomes cipher block chaining it looks more like this:

Source: Ervin Frenzel

PUBLIC KEY INFRASTRUCTURE (PKI)

The practical application of many variations of encryption is the Public Key Infrastructure (PKI). The infrastructure model provides assurances that an individual is who they claim to be. It works something like this; you assert who you are to a third party, the third party verifies who you are by making you prove your identity. Once you have proven who you are, they will now assert your identity to others on your behalf. When others question your digital identity, they send a request to the third party, who either validates or cannot validate your identity to the questioning individuals. The actual steps can be fairly complex, depending upon how the process is set up to run. Different organizations have different processes used to verify identities; both on the part of the organization who will be used to prove identities and the organization which chooses to assert its identity. It is best to ask your technicians which process is being implemented to fully understand how your organization or your provider will be set up to provide this service.

CONCLUSION

Encryption is no longer an option for organizations, it is a reality. Technicians and management need to work together to understand and implement it properly. While there are many ways to implement encryption, some are correct many are incorrect. Hashing produces a checksum to verify data, but is a one-way algorithm and there is no method to derive the data from the data hash. Symmetric or asymmetric encryption can be used to provide protection for your data, and provides a method which can be used to reveal what was once protected. Encryption can be enacted as streaming, block ciphers, or block chain ciphers. Your provider may require that you perform certain things as prove your identity. Once your identity is proven, your provider will act as a verifying or trusted agent to identify you.

QUESTIONS FOR FURTHER CONSIDERATION

1. Do you have a digital signature? If so how do you use it?

2. Explain how encryption is used behind the scenes for things that you do every day. How often do you use secure sites or encrypted sites when you use the Internet?

3. Thinking about encryption, can you think of encryption that was improperly implemented? Was it because of misunderstanding on the part of the corporation (either technicians or management) or was it caused by a system compromise?

4. Explain the difference in cost of implementation between streaming, block cipher, or cipher block chaining methods. Can multiple methods be used together? If so how?

REFERENCES

NISTIR 7298 Revision 2, Glossary of Key Information Security Terms. 2013. Information [Full Definition]. http://nvlpubs.nist.gov/nistpubs/ir/2013/NIST.IR.7298r2.pdf.

Tyson, Jeff. 2017. "How Encryption Works." HowStuffWorks: Tech. http://computer.howstuffworks.com/encryption3.htm

Wikibooks. 2016. "Cryptography/A Basic Public Key Example." https://en.wikibooks.org/wiki/Cryptography/A_Basic_Public_Key_Example

CHAPTER 6

NETWORKS: COMPUTERS WORKING WITH COMPUTERS

KEY WORDS

Bus Topology	ISP	Personal Area
Campus Area	Local Area Network	Network
Network	Logical Network	Physical Network
Client	Topologies	Topologies
Dark Web	Metropolitan Area	Server
Deep Web	Network	Wide Area Network
Intrusion Defense	Networks	
Systems	Network	
Intrusion Prevention	Vulnerabilities	
Systems		

INTRODUCTION TO NETWORKING

NETWORKS
Information system(s) implemented with a collection of interconnected components. Such components may include routers, hubs, cabling, telecommunications controllers, key distribution centers, and technical control devices.

Your computer is part of something larger—even if you are at home. A home computer, if it can get to the Internet or a network, is attached to a router or network interface device of some kind even if it is a wireless network. Your phone is a networked device as well, this doesn't matter whether you are on an old-fashioned analog phone or a new VoIP phone, to communicate (make and receive phone calls) the device has to be seen by the entire organization. Technically any two devices that communicate with each other are networked. So how does this actually break down? We break down **networks** based upon physical location, not necessarily physical size.

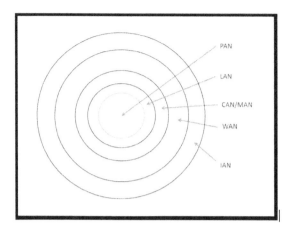

Source: Ervin Frenzel

PERSONAL AREA NETWORK
A computer network used for data transmission amongst devices such as computers, telephones, tablets, and personal digital assistants.

PHYSICAL NETWORK TOPOLOGIES
The way that the devices on a network are arranged and how they communicate with each other.

Personal Area Network (PAN)

The PAN is the most basic of all networks, even if you have not communicated with the network, but sent information to a physically attached printer (the trick is the printer is attached not through a network connection, but is directly connected) or used a wireless keyboard or mouse. So the shortest definition for a PAN (also called a **physical network**) is a computer and what is directly connected to it; this could even include a smartphone with a Bluetooth device or your smartphone to your vehicle.

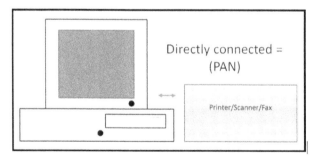

Source: Ervin Frenzel

LOCAL AREA NETWORK
A computer network that links devices within a building or group of adjacent buildings, especially one with a radius of less than 1 km.

Local Area Network (LAN)

This size network is the interconnection of several PANs. The easiest way to remember this is a small physical location where all devices share a common Internet gateway. The easiest way to determine if you share a common gateway is to navigate to www.whatismyip.com. This location will identify your Public IP address, the address that the rest of the world finds you through. Your ISP controls everything beyond your interface with them (your gateway). Think of your gateway as a house, and each device in the house is a separate room—so a shared street address (your public IP) but multiple rooms (your internal private IP's) inside. This format is shared across the neighborhood with the ISP issuing addresses to all of your neighbors, much like the post office provides the same street addresses.

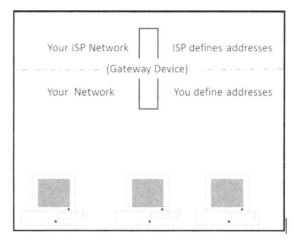

Source: Ervin Frenzel

Which really looks like this when it is distributed across multiple homes:

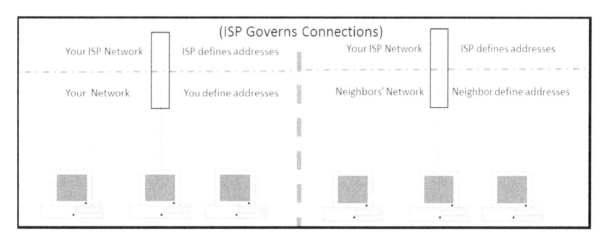

Source: Ervin Frenzel

Remember your network is part of your Internet Service Providers (ISP)'s network. So this is how to visualize this, if your local ISP is ANYISP.net but it purchased space from a major provider, MAJORPROVIDER.NET, who has a public range of IP's. Theoretically the major provider has a total of 256 IP addresses (which is a very small amount—they normally have tens of thousands more addresses to use), they divide their network up into multiple networks—ANYISP.net needs 128 addresses, a local hospital needs at least 56 addresses, a local advertising agency needs 25 addresses, and the list goes on. Eventually it narrows down to the individual user who needs an IP address, the same subdivision that went into MAJORPROVIDER.net goes into the ANYISP.net, only they have 128 addresses to break down. The breakdown for MAJORPROVIDER.net looks something like this:

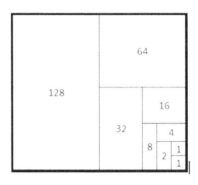

Source: Ervin Frenzel

Each network really is part of something bigger.

There are several different formations that a LAN may take. The concept of sharing computer resources is nothing new. The concept of sharing resources is older than humanity itself. As soon as it was discovered that a computer could actually work without having to have someone directing them constantly it became apparent that they could be organized much like any other organization, it had evolved into a real tool. Computers could be interconnected, but first we must understand that a computer by itself is much like a human being. It is a stand-alone system that can function and perform like a human being, but it has capabilities that can be increased by sharing resources with it. Computers are strong by themselves but stronger in groups. Computers were made to mimic mankind and how we communicate; after all the designers have lived in the physical world their entire lives. These designers, like anyone else in the environment, worked, played, and even fantasized in the real world. They naturally followed what they believed to be reality and in doing so changed our reality. These computers cannot just simply sit beside one another and talk to each other, they must be connected and form relationships (again physically mirroring human relationships). They are the perfect worker, but care must be taken to ensure they are listening to only their real boss. These relationships are networks, which we normally take for granted.

CONNECTING COMPUTERS

We place two processors on a system board to enhance a single machine, so why not expand the "system board" across several different devices, even across several different networks. We interconnect everything, when we connect two machines together we get a stronger device. When two devices work on the same problem it incrementally reduces the amount of time that any one device works to solve a problem. This thought process has extended processors into storage area networks (SANS) or network area storage (NAS) devices, recent developments have even gone so far as to reach across networks and share even screen saver processor time.[1] Online gaming platforms have shared resources for many years, but they also have shared threats. Currently gaming networks provide a rich hunting ground for attackers who look for weakly protected, over used networks. Many gamers willingly share resources between nodes across the state, across the nation, and even across the globe, completely unaware of the risks posed. Most home networks, where gaming occurs, are poorly protected at best; after all they are designed for gaming not for business class protection; but then again most business class networks are not designed to completely protect business class information.[2] Then again things are starting to look up; advances have been made to implement better security across many business cross sections, this includes resources shared between federal agencies, state agencies, local agencies, and business communities (both local and regional). Better cooperation between organizations means a better chance of defending information. When an organization defends its resources by itself it limits its defensive capability, when it works with other similar organizations information shared can make the difference between a successful defense and a compromised network with data lost. Think of it this way, a security guard working at a bank with no CCTV cameras, no weapon, no other security guards, and no means of notifying anyone else would be the equivalent of a stand-alone network monitor and have the same capability to notify others—essentially no additional support can be given or received. Now think of that same security guard (now armed) with integrated communications, being watched over by CCTV—which by the way is monitored remotely by multiple operators, next door to a police station. It's all about the diligence that can be delivered by those observing the network. This second scenario is much more inspiring and

1. Several government projects have gone down the technology sharing so much so that NIST has published information for sharing screen saver processor time across multiple networks. More information can be found at https://www.nist.gov/itl/math/screensaver-science.
2. An annual report published at https://pdf.ic3.gov/2015_IC3Report.pdf details much of the criminal activity that occurred during 2015. There is a separate report available for each of the preceding years available since the formation of the Internet Crime Complain Center (IC3) website.

better. It is much safer for everyone at the bank where things are being protected. Something to remember, an old military rule, never leave an obstacle where it cannot be observed (always observe your obstacles)—so you can learn your attacker's capability and know how long it takes for the attacker to overtake obstacles. The more obstacles that you emplace and the more eyes that can observe your obstacles, the better the chance you have of detecting and defeating those attempting to breach your bank. It may even be that some of those observing your obstacles are outside of your organization (those regional organizations that we spoke about earlier)—something to think about. Even managed security service providers can do this if you are short on resources.

NETWORKS

Computers communicate through networks, which can be through a physical wire (network or phone cable) or through the airwaves (used in wireless communication and cellular activity). Either way the communication

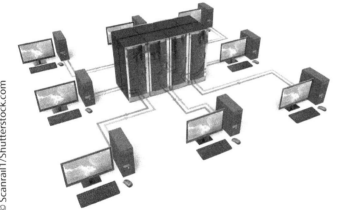

© Scanrail1/Shutterstock.com

path is how the computer talks to other computers just like when a person talks to another person. NIST defines a network as "Information system(s) implemented with a collection of interconnected components. Such components may include routers, hubs, cabling, telecommunications controllers, key distribution centers, and technical control devices" (Kissel 2013). Unfortunately that is only half the picture. This goes a long way in defining the physical but just like other relationships, this lacks the nuances of communication. Now, the bad news. Networks allow the interchange of information, both good and bad. Just like their human counterparts you can receive good news and bad news from your computer as it connects to another computer. You can also come into contact with things that can affect the availability of data.

When you walk into a fast-food restaurant or any other restaurant, how often do you think of the surroundings? When was the last time the restaurant counter was wiped down with disinfectant, what about the handrails leading to the counter, and worse what about the doorknobs getting into the restaurant? Did you notice the child using the handrail as a jungle gym after coming out of the bathroom (forgot to wash their hands), or the person who just wasn't feeling up to par and thought they could feed their way out of the "cold" that they were coming down with. I'm not here to make you never eat a lunch on the run again, but I am here to create awareness to what you encounter going anywhere. For that matter, when was the last time you actually cleaned off your cell phone (Castillo 2012)?[3] Your data faces very similar risks.

If you really think that your data is clean, think about the number of e-mails that you receive daily asking you to send money. How did they get your information to send you e-mails to begin with? Chances are an attacker received your information through either obtaining your e-mail address directly (you entered it into a website, or responded into an e-mail, signed up through a conference, etc.) or your information was obtained through a third party. Sad but true, you face challenges like this every day, and this is on a personal basis. When you look at the issue from a business point of view things get much worse; how many employees does the business have? Each employee brings their own issues with data, how cautious are they about where they look online, do they protect their passwords, do they work at home on machines where their kids just finished watching YouTube?[4]

Why network? Networks can be used for various reasons, but in general they serve one purpose—to save capital dollars. It is normally cheaper to pay for one resource and communicate between remote resources than it is to buy the resource multiple times. Take for instance a printer.[5] Let's say I have ten computers, as I have ten separate salespersons, located in a centralized office. The initial cost was $100 per printer (inexpensive bubble jet printers), each printer then requires four cartridges (black, cyan, magenta, and yellow) at $35 apiece. You now have an initial investment of $240 for each salesperson, $2,400 initially, which you have to use before the ink dries up (normally within a few weeks or months) and it disables the printer. The investment for ink will need to be made on average five times a year, at $140 per salesperson. This is assuming that the sales representatives only print about one hundred pages a month, the average month usage for a home user. Keep in mind I am not against bubble jet printers, they are great for the home user who doesn't need to print large volumes of information or who needs to only print one or two vacation photos at a time.

---

3. In 2012 Michelle Castillo reported for CBS Interactive, Inc that upward of 75 percent of cell phone users use their cell phone in the bathroom as a distraction of some kind, either to play games or initiate and receive phone calls.

4. YouTube is an online content delivery site which allows individuals to subscribe to channels for entertainment. The size of the organization and the content delivery from so many possible feeds limits the ability of Google, the parent organization, to prevent malicious code from being injected into content. Many useful feeds are found on the site; it has become a tool for delivery of personal and professional content. Because of the popularity of the site it has become a favorite location for attackers—much like a proverbial watering hole.

5. This is a hypothetical pricing, to demonstrate the cost savings associated with sharing resources.

The math looks something like this:

Initial printer cost	Initial ink cost	Ink upkeep cost	Extended cost per salesperson	Yearly cost for 10 salespersons
$100	$140	5 × $140	$940	$9,400

Now, assuming those ten sales reps are co-located in a small office space, let's look into a small to medium color laser printer. Let's assume an initial investment of $500, we can go after a decent printer for our sales reps. It might cost as high as $250 per cartridge and need four cartridges per quarter to maintain the cartridges, assuming heavy printing volume—about 3,000 sheets per month.

In this case the math looks something like this:

Initial printer cost	Initial ink cost	Ink upkeep cost	Yearly cost for 10 salespersons	Extended cost per salesperson
$500	$1,000	3 × $1,000	$4,500	$450

In essence these numbers reflect a perfect world, without having to replace equipment (i.e., ink jets) and it is not scaled to reflect the same 3,000 sheets per month. If you were to scale the bubble/ink jets to reflect 3,000 sheets a month the monthly cost would multiply by three. Currently only 1,000 sheets a month were scheduled for the ink jets. Additionally the printers would have to be replaced at least three times as they are not designed for the type of workload required to run the office.

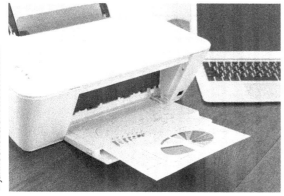

Now that we have looked at the original cost, the extended cost of the bubble jets would run a little over $28,200 a year. So we can see a clear savings at this point, but what about those pesky service calls for laser printers (which by the way I can do a lot of service calls for $23,700). We haven't even looked at the cost for time and efficiency savings for this small group. Numbers like these make it almost sensible to run an inexpensive color laser printer at home. More importantly it is important that savvy business owners and operators look at all of the expenses and options to lower the operating costs while maximizing profit for their organizations. Consider your home as the same type of organization and do the math—it may make more sense to buy a more expensive system for long-term ownership.

© jannoon028/Shutterstock.com

TYPES OF NETWORKS

Traditionally there are several different physical structures of networks. We might use a bus, ring, star, or a hybrid (combination)[6] architectures. To make it worse we also organize these networks into logical connection types such as the point-to-point or mesh topology. The easiest way to remember the difference between these concepts is that physical structures describe how the devices physically connect to the network, while the logical structure describes how we organize our connections.

So who will be talking? And how will they talk without talking over one another? Like any conversation there has to be two entities involved in a conversation—one to talk, the other to listen. To be successful the two must change roles at some time during the conversation. Typically we classify those entities/devices as either **clients** (something that requests something from another) or **servers** (something that answers a request from clients). Technically the "client" is an "individual or process acting on behalf of an individual who makes requests of a guard or dedicated server. The client's requests to the guard or dedicated server can involve data transfer to, from, or through the guard or dedicated server" (Kissel 2013, 32). Servers are a little more difficult to define, as they can be anything that answers a request from a client. In a peer to peer network each device can be both a client and a server to every other device on the network. We organize these conversations into Peer to Peer (referred to as Ad Hoc when wireless) or Client/Server conversations (Kissel 2013).

NETWORK PHYSICAL ARCHITECTURES

Bus Topology

A **bus topology** is fairly straightforward, it is basically a line between and connecting multiple machines. Today this might exist when a computer directly connects to another computer for file transfer through a single wire. Though these networks typically have multiple machines that connect to them, they have an identified start and end. This network is fairly secure in that a break in the line in either direction will identify a loss of continuity and shut down all data flow (in some cases only the data flow past the point of breakage). In which case, troubleshooting is performed by moving the termination device to the next link until the remaining section of network works again.

CLIENT
A piece of computer hardware or software that accesses a service made available by a server.

SERVER
A computer program or a device that provides functionality for other programs or devices, called "clients."

BUS TOPOLOGY
A line between and connecting multiple machines.

---

6. Various networking organizations or authors will add to or subtract from the types of physical structures, but these are the generally accepted structures within the network architecture fields.

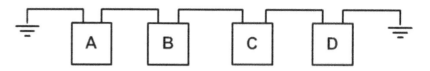

Source: Ervin Frenzel

Ring Topology

A ring topology is identified by having neither a beginning nor an end node; all nodes are connected to the next so that each device has only two physical connections. This keeps the network somewhat small as the data has to pass from one device to the next listening to determine if the traffic is for that device. Traffic will flow in one direction to assist with computers not talking over each other. Again this network topology is fairly secure, but also fairly vulnerable, in that a break in the line will shut down communications for the entire ring.

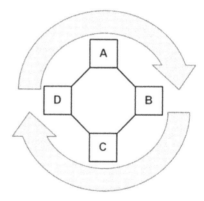

Source: Ervin Frenzel

Star Topology

A star topology is physically centered on a device (a hub, switch, or even a wireless access point) that provides a connection point for client devices to connect into. The strength of this design is that any device except the centralized point of the star can fail and not affect the rest of the devices. Devices can be added or removed without affecting the data flow, but this also becomes a weakness when it comes to security, as another device can be added without detection while not affecting the information flow. Troubleshooting is extremely simple as the down device is the one experiencing a problem (could be the device or the connection to the centralized device).

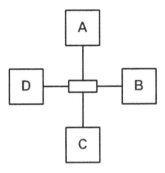

Source: Ervin Frenzel

Hybrid Topology

The final physical topology is of course the hybrid topology. This topology has no "defined" layout as it is whatever is needed as the network grows. Part of it may be a bus topology, part of it may interconnect to ring topology through a star network. This network often evolves as an organization evolves, so almost any variation of configuration is possible.

LOGICAL NETWORK TOPOLOGIES

LOGICAL NETWORK TOPOLOGIES
The arrangement of devices on a computer network and how they communicate with one another.

Logical network topologies can and often do mirror physical topologies, so many of the topologies discussed will seem similar to what has already been discussed. This is because, again, system designers tend to stay with what they understand.

Point to Point

This involves simply connecting two devices. Not much more explanation is required, it starts at "A" and goes to "B."

Source: Ervin Frenzel

Point to Multipoint

This variation of a point to point network involves connecting "A" to "B," then "A" to "C" (without going through "B"). This is repeated until all network required network connections are made. Logically each connection is a point to point connection, physically this is a variation of a star topology.

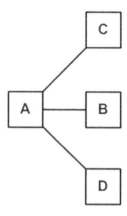

Source: Ervin Frenzel

Multipoint to Multipoint

Redundant links are created between key locations to provide backup connectivity in case of a primary link failure. It can also be used to isolate
traffic from a given point to another point, while preventing specific traffic
from going through what might be an otherwise unwanted route. There is
not a redundant link between all sites, so some sites may suffer in case of
an outage. This method can be fairly expensive as an organization will have
to be prepared to pay for multiple links to certain sites.

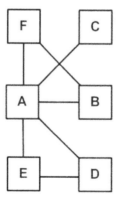

Source: Ervin Frenzel

Mesh Topology

Mesh topology is the most expensive of all. Logically this is the topology of
a peer to peer network. There is a formula to help scale this network, but
keep in mind that while you can physically connect any number of devices
there may be limitations imposed by applications and software.[7] The formula to determine the number of physical connections is n(n–1)/2 or the

---

7. Microsoft supports a maximum number of ten devices on a peer to peer network for Windows
XP and twenty devices on peer to peer networks that are all Windows 7 or higher.

number of devices times the number of devices minus 1 then divide the resultant by 2. A Windows 7 peer to peer network containing 20 devices would have 20(19)/2 or 190 connections involved. Each device could act as a client for one device but answer request (become a server) for another device—this is why there are imposed limitations as this would require large amounts of individual system resources (Ram and processor capabilities) on every system.

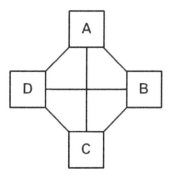

Source: Ervin Frenzel

SYSTEM VULNERABILITIES

Vulnerabilities start with people; they have bad habits or patterns within their life that can be observed and exploited. An individual user has had an entire lifetime of experience that has colored their perception of reality, these are of course different for every individual. That is part of our strength and ultimately part of our greatest weakness as a species. Each individual believes that they are the only experts that they know in their life about their life, and in regard to their individual experience they are correct. A designer who designed the system had either worked with someone else who shaped their thoughts about system design or had experience designing systems. The programmer who wrote the Operating System code that runs on the system experienced a very similar situation, each application programmer experienced the same thing. Strangely each of them believes that they did the absolute best that they could, as they should (if they really took the time to build the system the way they wanted to). Will the next iteration be better? Of course. Will it have the same or similar thought processes involved? You bet.

So far we have looked at why do we implement networks, and how do we design our logical and physical topologies. We have not looked at how vulnerabilities are spread by networks. Let's look at this now. Remember those ten sales reps, let's use them as an example again and let's create a history and a profile for each of them. The company started out working slowing with only two salespersons, initially they had Windows XP Professional on their systems but as the business grew they received Windows 7 Professional machines. The Windows XP machines were put into storage and eventually handed down to the next two salespersons who came on board. We now have four sales reps, with varying types of computers. The company decided to push for expansion, which they did—they added six sales reps, each received a Windows 8.1 machine so that they could effectively reach out to clients during this period of rapid growth. A quick inventory of equipment shows that we now have two Windows XP Professional machines, two Windows 7 Professional machines, and six Windows 8.1 machines. None of these machines were designed to be in their business environment in that the company has not yet implemented a Client/Server network. So the machines are currently in a peer to peer network configuration.

Think of a computer as a complete system, similar to a human being—there are things that are similar between all human beings at least at the physical level which shows patterns between people. For example, typically we recognize that others have or should have two arms and two legs, we should have a head on our shoulders, a heart, lungs, and certain internal organs. This could make us any number of species, thus we have been categorized as within the animal kingdom. We, however, have been classified as part of the human species and can expect certain things about other members of our own species. We have found that we are prone to cancer, influenza, colds, and even breaking of bones. We see genetic anomalies, such as sickle cell anemia that plague members of our species but not all of us. The same things can be said for computers and operating systems. A vulnerability found in Windows might affect all operating systems created by Microsoft, for desktops and even servers. Let's consider the computer and the user as a complete system.

The importance of having a computer updated cannot be over emphasized. Computer vulnerabilities are discovered daily for operating systems that are currently supported by their developers. Just because a computer operating system is no longer supported by its developers doesn't mean that vulnerabilities stop being identified. According to Nayak, Marino, Efstathopoulos, and Dumitras (n.d.), Windows XP had approximately 45 million lines of code, Windows 7 had more than 50 million lines of code. Many of the lines of code are reused from one operating system to the next, so a weakness found in one operating system can often be found in another especially if written by the same organization, for example Microsoft. As a rule it is cheaper to reuse software and improve upon it than it is to write a program from scratch. That being said, if a developer wrote code for OS "A," then they will bring those same habits and designs into OS "B." Professional security practitioners look for patterns and repetition to see how that can be leveraged to create an opportunity. They rarely find a single event that provides the exploit opportunity of a lifetime, an opportunity to gain information that you as a business owner would not want them to have. This is exactly the methodology that an attacker takes to gain an advantage in your computer, network, or business. More importantly these patterns are caused by the designers who design and build systems and operating systems, intentionally for ease of support and as a point of reference when working with the systems later on.

The Windows XP and Windows 7 machines no longer receive updates from Microsoft as these operating systems are not being updated—it is like having a disease or illness that no more research is going into to fix. The sales reps indicated that they did not have time to wait for the updates when they were trying to earn a living working with clients, this introduces a vulnerability that is external to your system itself. So now we can see vulnerabilities in the system, in the operating system, and with the user, but wait that is not all. When we network our systems we are now exposed to the vulnerabilities from other systems. Remember we consider a computer and a user together as a system. If another user opens a virus on their system, your system could be exposed. More importantly we are exposed to all of the bad habits that their system has. Will all of their bad habits be equivalent to the Black Plague? No, more than likely their bad habits will have the impact of a head cold, but some of those habits can be the equivalent of the plague—the question is will the vaccine be given prior to exposure or will the system be harmed from exposure. These are known vulnerabilities and exposures, but what about those that you don't know about. Keep in mind you probably do not think about the exposure that you have every day, but do you really understand the exposures that you do not know about? Attackers want information that you have. The question is how far are they willing to go to get it. Worse, attackers are willing to use whatever means possible to get this, they will attack the system (the user, the operating system, and the physical device itself) to get what they want.

Good news, you are not alone in identifying system vulnerabilities, nor are you alone in defending your system. System updates are critical, but they are not limited to updates of your operating system, even though defenders often only think in these terms. We usually consider questions such as, What operating system? Which applications? but we tend to forget about the hardware. The hardware itself may need to be updated. Keeping your system updated is like receiving a natural vaccine against so many variations of the common cold or letting your immune system develop.

Anti-virus programs and updates are designed to protect against viruses (even though there will be ones that cannot be protected against).[8]

BACK TO NETWORK TYPES

CAMPUS AREA NETWORK

A computer network made up of an interconnection of local area networks (LANs) within a limited geographical area.

METROPOLITAN AREA NETWORK

Is similar to a local area network (LAN) but spans an entire city or campus. MANs are formed by connecting multiple LANs.

Campus Area Network or **Metropolitan Area Network** (CAN or MAN)— The third major size category is the CAN or MAN. This network includes multiple LAN networks, each floor of a building could be a LAN and with multi-story buildings (say five or more) suddenly we have a small CAN. On the other hand if we were to have multiple buildings with a LAN in each building, and the buildings were spread across a small geographic area (even if it physically extends outside of a city limits) we might identify this as a MAN. Another key difference is that the CAN still provides the ability to control the interconnects between multiple LANs (you have multiple LANs behind your gateway).

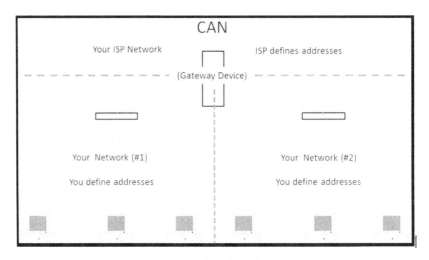

Source: Ervin Frenzel

If you control it, if it is local it is generally considered a type of local area network (LAN) or a Campus Area Network or Metropolis Area Network (CAN or MAN); however, with a CAN you still can control the interconnecting networks (they are behind your common gateway). You might have fiber or copper lines between buildings, or cabling between building

---

8. A note here is that much like a human being there can only be one antivirus. Having more than one is much like having an autoimmune disease. It normally makes the system fight against itself and wastes precious resources.

ISP
Internet Service Provider.

floors but have a common interface with your **ISP**—this is a CAN. The MAN however allows you to control the networks behind different gateways, but your ISP or multiple ISPs provide the interconnectivity of your networks. This is really the beginning of a WAN.

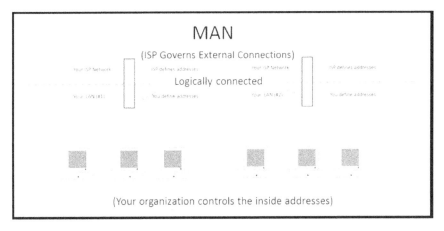

Source: Ervin Frenzel

WIDE AREA NETWORK
A computer network in which the computers connected may be far apart, generally having a radius of more than 1 km.

Wide Area Network (WAN)—This is a compilation of multiple smaller networks, it covers many different types of networks. It may have LANs, CANs, or MANs. The difference is again geography. These networks are not regional, they may have networks in Europe, North and South America, Africa, or Asia. These networks are much like an extended MAN, you own the inside but your connections are managed by one or more ISPs. Simply put the organization is all over the place, quite literally.

Now we need to discuss "what is the Internet, really?"

We know that the data and hardware we control is really internal to our LAN, and what others control is really external to our LAN. What if we now work for a different company? For Company B, their LAN is now external to Company A's internal LAN, so there is a clear differentiation. We can now look at internal versus external network. Most of everything we have looked at so far would be internal to our network, after all we still own all of the traffic, data, and all (even though we may not own the routes used).

External traffic is destined to travel to a place that we do not own or have a right to control.

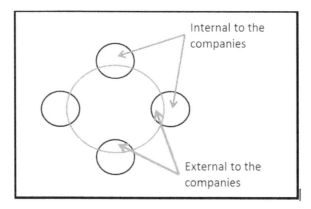

Source: Ervin Frenzel

What you do not see in this demonstration is that the interconnections are an extended star, which looks like this:

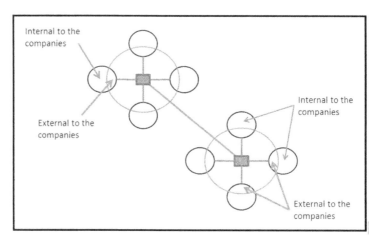

Source: Ervin Frenzel

This is the basis for the Internet, the external connections and data shared between multiple sites. Of course there are many millions more connections and interconnections that cannot be shown on this page. Companies choose what goes into the public space versus staying in the private space. The public information is of course the data that can be searched via the web and with various web search tools. Notice that there is a significant amount of difference between the external and the internal data amounts. This is not an accident. Companies need to protect their intellectual data, so it is not shared in the public space.

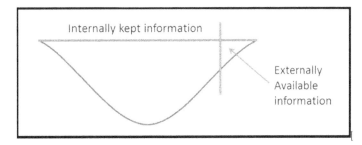

Source: Ervin Frenzel

This model assumes that the company does not wish to share some internal information with corporate partners without sharing all of their internal information. This is the basis for the "deep" web, which provides "trusted" partners with information as demonstrated by this model:

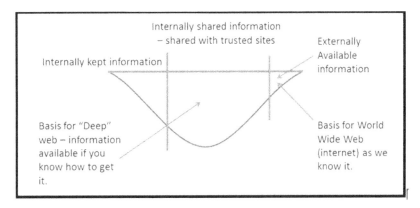

Source: Ervin Frenzel

So how does one become trusted, have a corporate agreement or some other method of gaining access (legally), such as having a relationship with a company that trusts the other company. This extended "trust" is basically the "deep" web and provides an incredible amount of data.[9] The data includes information about browsing habits of individuals, groups, data analysis of just about everything, and information that is not generally available to the public. Interesting enough many organizations track user activity on their externally (publicly) available sites, without users knowing that they are being tracked.[10] It is assumed that use constitutes consent when it comes to tracking activity. This applies to almost every organization that offers externally available information. Not all organizations are

9. In 2014, CNN reported that publicly available websites accounted for about 1 percent of the web as we know it, the rest would be considered Deep or Dark Web. Additional information available at: http://money.cnn.com/2014/03/10/technology/deep-web/.
10. There are ways to keep some of your information private, such as going to myactivity.google.com which allows users to opt out of being tracked by the Google corporation.

DEEP WEB
Anything on the Internet which is not indexed by a search engine.

the same, there are political organizations, economic organizations, commercial activities, Non-Government Organizations (NGOs), government organizations, military organizations, and others. There are even organizations that specialize in things that mainstream society considers taboo. This area of the **deep web**, which is not generally accessible, is considered to be the "dark" web.

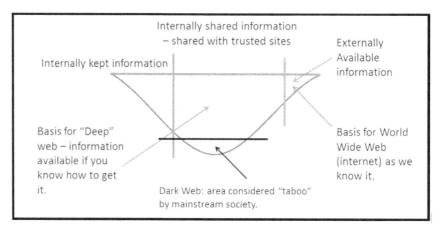

Source: Ervin Frenzel

DARK WEB
A subset of the deep web, which requires special software and/or authorization to access.

INTRUSION PREVENTION SYSTEMS
A network security/threat prevention technology that examines network traffic flows to detect and prevent vulnerability exploits.

INTRUSION DEFENSE SYSTEMS
A device or software application that monitors a network or systems for malicious activity or policy violations.

This book is not designed to identify the portals to the dark or the deep web, just to raise awareness to their existance and that you will need special tools to access these types of sites. Many organizations go out of their way to block access to both deep or **dark web**, and rightfully so, as external organizations may not want you or those who work for you to have access to their shared information. They take many of the same precautions that ordinary sites take to protect their data and networks, they use active defenses such as **Intrustion Prevention Systems (IPS)** and detect unwanted tresspassers through **Intrusion Defense Systems (IDS)**. They perform all of the same administration procedures as an administrator of a general site.

The deep web requires access through a deep web portal or site which oftentimes is not even available through normal browsers such as Internet Explorer, Chrome, or even Mozilla[11] such as Shodan or other specialized search engines.[12] Dark websites will often build defenses to defend their sites, to include malcode installed on their websites, active couter attacking mechanisms, and other methods. In essence dark websites really do not want you to to visit.

---

11. Internet Explorer, Chrome, and Mozilla Firefox are protected by copyrights by their respective copyright holders.
12. More information about Shodan, which has been described as "scary" is available at http://money.cnn.com/2013/04/08/technology/security/shodan/?iid=EL.

Now the why, there are communications standards or "protocols" that direct this traffic to and from the destinations but not all protocols operate the same way.

HOW DOES TRAFFIC KNOW IF IT IS LAN OR WAN TRAFFIC?

First let's look at the two basic types of protocols, they can be classified as "routed" or "routing." As their name suggests one set of protocol types provides the navigation system for the other. Routing protocols flow between interconnecting devices known as "routers" essentially providing the traffic control solution that provides warning in case of network congestion, outages, or addition of routes. Routed protocols can be compared to semi tractors that have a payload in the trailer. In essence, the Internet as a whole is a virtual copy of a physical transportation network and it has all the same control components except in the virtual world.

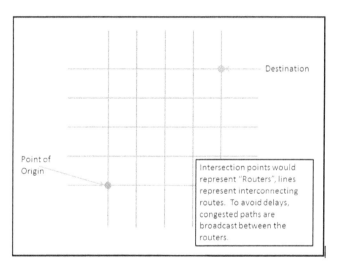

Source: Ervin Frenzel

NETWORK VULNERABILITIES
A weakness which allows an attacker to reduce a system's information assurance. Vulnerability is the intersection of three elements: a system susceptibility or flaw, attacker access to the flaw, and attacker capability to exploit the flaw.

Of course actual Internet connections are not as evenly spaced as street intersections. Some are further apart, some are extemely close, other connections have huge amounts of bandwidth. Recent "road work" may have some routes down for maintenance, or restored previously down interconnects.

NETWORK VULNERABILITIES

So far a lot of work has gone into explaining how networks work and even how they expand our capabilities, but when we look at them we forget something critical—capabilities are vulnerabilities. There is a model called by Caltagirone, Pendergast, and Betz (2016) the "Diamond model of intrusion analysis," which is based upon four components: the attacker, capabilities, infrastructure, and finally the victim. Interestingly enough there is no distinction upon who owns the infrastructure or who owns the capabilities, but it is only based upon the thought that the attacker and the victim have to be linked through either capabilitiy or infrastructure. What does that mean to you? Your infrastructure can easily become an attacker's infrastructure, it all depends upon the preparation that each side has taken in advance. If you are properly prepared you may be able to defend your infrastructure. If not, the attacker may own it before you even know that it was compromised. We highly recommend that you spend some time researching this if it is something you might want to learn more about. No one says you need to be the expert, but like good managers it might be beneficial to gain some professional expertise by obtaining those persons (or growing internally) to better assist your organization.

VULNERABILITY REMEDIATIONS

We would be lying if we said you can remediate every vulnerability. In fact, we would be lying if we said you could identify every vulnerability, but this is the challenge of data/network security professionals everywhere. Many modern attempts at redesigning software focus on stopping vulnerabilities before they get placed into production software. Remember, according to NISTIR 7298, Revision 2, Glossary of Key Information Security Terms a vulnerability is:

> Weakness in an information system, system security procedures, internal controls, or implementation that could be exploited or triggered by a threat source.
>
> SOURCE: SP 800-53; SP 800-53A; SP 800-37; SP 800-60; SP 800-115; FIPS 200
>
> A weakness in a system, application, or network that is subject to exploitation or misuse. (SOURCE: SP 800-61)
>
> Weakness in an information system, system security procedures, internal controls, or implementation that could be exploited by a threat source. (SOURCE: CNSSI-4009)

Vulnerabilities exist that only an attacker (who uncovered the vulnerability) and the programmer are aware of. In many instances the programmer is also unaware of the vulnerability, because they have been taught to program in a certain way, use a particular program, use a particular hardware platform, a specific protocol, or use a software library for convenience. As you can see, it is fairly easy to stack the deck against defenders.

Now the good news. In the past very little attention was spent in preparing a defense for a network, today that is not the case. Defenders have allies. Defenders have lots of allies, they are starting to organize defenses and coordinate between organizations. Let's break this down into two main factors: what you (or your organization) can do, and what others can do to assist you.

WHAT YOU CAN DO

Let's start with users and how we can fix issues that they might have.

1. Implement policies and enforce them
2. Use passphrases
3. Scan your software for unknown issues (Audit)
4. Scan your network for unknown issues (Audit)
5. Patch your software
6. Use antivirus software (endpoint and network level)
7. Segment your network
8. Encrypt your traffic

Review your policies and determine which policies need to be updated. No policy is perfect, no matter how much it has been tweaked. If you are at home, review what you do to protect your own data. If you are at work, take the time to identify what should be protected. This process may take the form of an official risk management survey, reviewing results from an external audit, or it may take the form of directives coming from leadership.

Of course the most basic is a password—Right? Don't use passwords, use passphrases, for example "TheBlueFox" might be an acceptable passphrase, but it might need to be expanded to meet complexity requirements. It might end up looking like "+h3B1ueF0X" or some other variation—this particular phrase has upper and lower case alphabet characters "hueBFX"as well as special characters "+" and numbers "310." The original password might have been sufficiently long (10 characters)—which also typically meets sufficient length requirements, but some networks might have more stringent password length requirements. This is the first real thing that can be done to harden your systems.

The second major thing that should be done is scanning your system (individual and network). Find out where you have known vulnerabilities, they will appear on endpoints and network devices. This should be done on a regular basis, after the first scan you should be able to determine if the scanning software is working appropriately for you—if the software isn't what you are expecting then you might need to continue looking for software that fits your needs. You may be surprised to learn what really exists in this space, especially if you have never seen a scan of your network or end points. There are many different software suites to help you with this, some are free while others are licensed and must be purchased.

Now patch your system. Many manufacturers test their software or have vulnerabilities reported to them which they correct and software patches sent out to legitimate subscribers. Register your software, stay current with patches or at least as far as you can without causing other software to fail or cause other vulnerabilities in other software suites. This last warning is very real. A software patch from one company may disable software from another company. The patch could be antivirus software or it could be blocked by default. This patching includes operating systems (OS), applications, antivirus software, and even software that you discover after you do your initial scan. Keep in mind this last class of software might be called "shadow IT" in some arenas.[13]

The question is how can you track all of the devices on your network? Segmenting your network is a very simple answer to a very complex problem. In essence you reduce traffic. When you make your networks smaller (aka segmenting them), you can better observe changes in them and you can also detect changes planned or unplanned. This also prevents prying eyes from seeing more than they should.

© jannoon028/Shutterstock.com

Encrypt your traffic. Let's look at what this does, or rather what it conceals. If our network has plain text information traversing it, anyone who is able to see the network technically can see that information. So what do you have traveling across your network that you might not want others to see? The answer

---

13. Shadow IT is a term that has been showing up for several years. It refers to software or capabilities that are not officially sanctioned by an organization, but whose capability is depended upon by the organization to accomplish day-to-day tasks. The technology typically is not under the control of the organization, but is under control of users.

is you will never know. The receptionist just decided to purchase something for her grandkids, the CEO is sending information about a proposed merger, and worse the annual stock report (which has yet to be approved) is floating around the network. Would any of those things cause you to lose sleep at night if the information were exposed? All of it should. So encrypt the traffic, apply a lock to prevent honest people from prying, and keep dishonest people from getting a chance to pry. Not all traffic should be encrypted though, but with the recent changes in network traffic more traffic will need to be encrypted.

WHAT OTHERS CAN DO

Now you have a better view of what you have, after all you have scanned your network, scanned your devices, and patched software so that few pieces of software have vulnerabilities (OK, this last part might be a bit of a stretch). So the list is fairly short for what others can do to assist you in your tasks.

1.   Have your network audited

2.   Talk with peer organizations

3.   Talk with your ISP

4.   Talk with local law enforcement

5.   Network your security professionals and managers

Step one for what others can do is, of course, have your network audited. This is not a punishment piece. Auditing is a confirmation that you are doing the right thing or at least following the steps that you said you were going to do (keep in mind company policies are what they should be evaluated against). If policies create gaps, then address the policies; if management creates the gap, then address management; if technicians are the gap, then address the technicians. An audit should be used as a guide to improve your network and your security, don't blow off the results or let it get buried—someone paid money to have the audit done. Learn from it.

Step two is equally important. Talk with peer organizations. If you are in banking look to other banks (or bank groups). If you are in health care work with other health care organizations. Bottom line is simple: like business functions can learn from one another. Administrators will face similar functions and challenges, management will see similar challenges. Now for the down side of this one, when your administrators interact with other organizations they may exchange more than just knowledge that you want exchanged. They may exchange payscales and other bits of information that you may not want exchanged. Advise your technicians and administrators what they can rightfully talk about and what should be avoided.

Let your ISP know what your plans are. After all during an attack they will see it first, during audits they will again see it first. They have the ability to offset many of the things that you cannot—they might even be able to mitigate attacks that you cannot.

Talk with local, state, and federal law enforcement. They can talk to you about current trends that they see not just in your local town or state, but also what they see happening on a much larger scale. For example, health care organizations may suddenly watch for more ransomware attacks, or they may need to purchase bitcoin in advance in case of an attack. Some hacker organizations have now established that they are not going to attack health care organizations as it can kill people, but this is not a reason to relax standards.[14] Attackers are no longer attacking blindly, they know who they will initiate attacks on and they are looking for cash money. The larger the organization the more likely they will become a target, if they have not already. As advances are made smaller organizations will provide just as rich targets.

Network your staff. Let them attend professional conferences. They need the bigger picture. If an administrator says they don't need the bigger picture—then they are doing you a disservice. Analysts and administrators need to know the picture so they can tell management what is out there and what new trends are showing up.

CONCLUSION

Just like traffic systems in a city, there are those who want to watch the traffic flow as it occurs and it keeps track of traffic as it flows. These systems like to gather that information and sell it to those who want to identify your browsing patterns. In a recent article about Google's behavior it was identified that Google was doing just that, of course they are not the only ones.[15] Other organizations and state agencies do it as well, in fact there are a great many different groups that want to know what you do when you browse the web for academic and other reasons.

There are several ways that traffic is identified as entering a network to stay local or entering the network to leave the network. First we have the

---

14. Not all hackers are blind attackers, some know their targets before they attack and select whether to initiate the attack. http://www.zdnet.com/article/hackers-split-on-ethics-of-ransom ware-attacks-on-hospitals/

15 http://www.theregister.co.uk/2016/09/14/google_location_location_location/

concept of private versus public addresses. When Internet addressing first came out, it was a free-for-all. As time progressed it was discovered that there was more demand for the access to the Internet, but there were roughly 4.3 billion addresses (or 2 to the 32nd power for an exact number). This would have worked except that many addresses were required to create the interconnections that bind the Internet together, many more were not being used because of our previous example.

QUESTIONS FOR FURTHER CONSIDERATION

1. Map out the computer system you currently use at home. What type of network are you using?

2. At your work place do you use a common printer, or individual printers? What type of network is this?

3. Do you maintain a part of your computer hard drive that is separate from that available for public access through a LAN? Would you consider this to be "dark" web material? What about at work?

4. What types of protective systems do you have in place at work to identify and prevent penetration by those wanting to access your computer network? Is it effective?

REFERENCES

Caltagirone, S., A. Pendergast, and C. Betz. 2016. Diamond Model of Intrusion Analysis. http://www.activeresponse.org/wp-content/uploads/2013/07/diamond.pdf.

Castillo, M. 2012. Survey: 75 percent of Americans admit to using phone while in bathroom. http://www.cbsnews.com/news/survey-75-percent-of-americans-admit-to-using-phone-while-in-bathroom.

Kissel, R. (Ed.) 2013. NIST IR 7298 Revision 2, *Glossary of Key Information Security Terms.* http://dx.doi.org/10.6028/NIST.IR.7298r2

Nayak, K., D. Marino, P. Efstathopoulos, and T. Dumitras. (nd). Some Vulnerabilities Are Different Than Others; Studying Vulnerabilities and Attack Surfaces in the Wild. https://www.cs.umd.edu/~kartik/papers/1_vuln.pdf.

NISTIR 7298 Revision 2, Glossary of Key Information Security Terms. 2013. Vulnerability [Full Definition]. http://nvlpubs.nist.gov/nistpubs/ir/2013/NIST.IR.7298r2.pdf.

CHAPTER 7

PROTECTING COMPUTER ENTERPRISES

KEY WORDS

Hardware	Software	Threats
Patch Management	Vulnerabilities	Vulnerabilities

TESTING AND VERIFICATION—DISCLAIMER

Remember legally we can only test a system, it is a crime in most countries/states to attack a system and it could fall under multiple international, federal, and state laws. Before testing any system ensure that there is a written document which states what can and cannot be done with a system signed by the individual responsible for the system (owner). This cannot be signed by the user if the user does not own the device.

This is a general flow of how things work; threats exist on your system, when they are scanned and identified they are identified as vulnerabilities, once a vulnerability is exploited (for testing purposes it is now a penetration test). It is important to emphasize that you must have permission before testing any system, not just any permission but written permission stating exactly what you can and cannot test. If you exceed the authority granted you, you may be guilty of a crime. If you fail to fulfill the requirements you may also be held liable for breach of contract. Make sure that if you are tasked with testing a system you take the time and effort to work this through an attorney who really understands what you must do and the steps involved in doing it.

Audits are conducted either by a third party or by an independent group within your organization. Again, vulnerabilities already exist. A vulnerability scan simply reveals that they exist, no attempt to exploit or take advantage of the vulnerability occurs. Once a vulnerability is exploited, you either have an authorized penetration test or an attack. An authorized exploitation by an authorized penetration tester means that everything is identified, documented (recorded in the appropriate format), revealed to the appropriate persons if critical enough, exploited, identified how to remediate issue, and brought back to a functioning status following the penetration test. If the penetration tester does not follow these basic steps they could actually be conducting an unauthorized penetration test (an attack), even though they had permission to perform the initial penetration test.

UNDERSTANDING THREATS

THREATS
Anything that can exploit a vulnerability, intentionally or accidentally, and obtain, damage, or destroy an asset.

This definition raises a few questions such as what is a **threat** and how will I recognize a threat? And finally, are all threats going to be realized? Threats are not vulnerabilities; they are the possibility that someone or something can adversely affect your system. We look to NIST to identify what exactly is a threat.

> 1.) Any circumstance or event with the potential to adversely impact organizational operations (including mission, functions, image, or reputation), organizational assets, individuals, other organizations, or the Nation through an information system via unauthorized access, destruction, disclosure, modification of information, and/or denial of service. 2.) The potential source of an adverse event. 3.) Any circumstance or event with the potential to adversely impact organizational operations (including mission, functions, image, or reputation), organizational assets, or individuals through an information system via unauthorized access, destruction, disclosure, modification of information, and/or denial of service. Also, the potential for a threat-source to successfully exploit a particular information system vulnerability.

Once we know what the threats are we can plan for a defense against those threats.

PLANNING A DEFENSE

As we look at our systems, data, and interactions we must plan how we and others interact with our systems. It is easiest if we break our data and systems into zones. I prefer to identify separate zones, these zones are named for what they actually are. While this list is not all-inclusive, it provides a starting point for what we need to address. Webster's defines a "system" as "Any organized assembly of resources and procedures united and regulated by interaction or interdependence to accomplish a set of specific functions." Let's build a picture of our system. We will address weaknesses and strengths after we discuss the main groups that should be tested.

Let's start with endpoints (the thing that almost everyone knows), after all we work with them every day—right? We can then work our way out to the Internet and address the vulnerabilities that we can seldom even think about. Some of the endpoints presented will surprise you as you know they exist, but may not normally think of them.

Endpoints

- ► PC's
- ► Mac clients
- ► Linux clients
- ► Printers
- ► Scanners
- ► TV's
- ► Kiosks (little computers where customers can enter online inquiries)
- ► CCTV cameras
- ► DVR's
- ► Credit card machines
- ► Other embedded devices
- ► Bluetooth devices connected to endpoints
- ► Any device that people directly interact with

© tuthelens/Shutterstock.com

Network Devices

- Hubs
- Switches
- Can be non-perimeter routers

Interconnectivity Devices

- Routers
- VPN concentrators
- Modems
- Multiplexers

Infrastructure

- Servers
  - Proxy (Internet access, file inspection, anti-virus, update systems, communications)
  - File and Printer
  - Web servers
  - DataBase servers
- Storage Area Network (SAN) systems
- Security systems (logging system, IPS/IDS, scanning system—such as Rapid7 and others, authentication servers and associated devices)

Communication Systems

- Telecommunication
- VoIP
- E-mail
- Skype
- Unified Communications

Web Interfaces

- Websites
- FTP servers
- Open network/Internet ports

Applications

Publicly Available Information

Weaknesses Created through Misconfiguration Of:

► Devices

► Software

► Connections

Hardware and System/Subsystem Attack Footprints

All of the previously mentioned systems have common features. Once again let's look at the requirements to be a computer. Remember, according to Merriam Webster computers are "programmable usually electronic device that can store, retrieve, and process data" (Computer [Def. 2, Full definition], n.d.). The previously listed devices are all actually computers or run on specially built computers—let me explain. A computer is actually built for a specific purpose, in the case of an endpoint, even in a printer there is a processor, memory, a system board, and specific **hardware** that contains instructions for the device.

HARDWARE
the electro-mechanical components and external attachments used to effectively connect operating systems.

OK, so we have identified where to look but now we must address what to look for and where we can find additional information to assist us in this search. It may be hard to imagine but a system looks somewhat like this.

Source: Ervin Frenzel

Let's now look at a computer as a system of systems. The system board is in fact an independent system, which becomes a platform to create an even larger system and even hosts other systems. The system board attaches to a hard drive, and has other systems that sit on it. The video system (which has a processor, memory, input and output capabilities—making it a complete system) is one such system. What makes this even more difficult to defend is that each processor is a complete system by itself as well. The processor performs specific functions and is programmed with logic; this allows the processor to do what is asked of it. This is a visual of how a system is a system of systems.

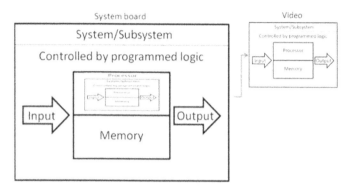

Source: Ervin Frenzel

A keyboard, mouse, or other input device may not qualify as a separate system but they are input devices nonetheless; a Bluetooth device or any other networked device that inputs to a system might easily qualify as a system in and of itself. Looking at each system/subsystem reveals weaknesses and strengths that might otherwise be overlooked. Any input device could cause a system compromise.[1] The concept is simple—input compromised data and I do not have to compromise the whole system, as I can easily predict how the system should respond (after all it has been programmed to respond in a certain manner according to the initially programmed logic).

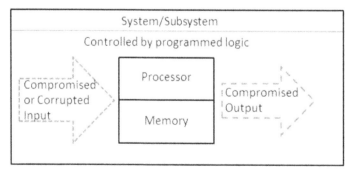

Source: Ervin Frenzel

---

1. One such example of an input causing a compromise can be found at https://www.cnet.com/news/i-got-mousejacked/. Leaving any Bluetooth device on and actively searching for a paired device leaves any system waiting to be compromised.

Notice that the Processor and Memory are not compromised, they are in fact still functioning as they are supposed to. This predictability is exactly why and what the compromised output should be. As we refer back to a previous section remember that integrity deals with preventing unauthorized changes or modifications, either accidental or intentional. This is not always the case though; other compromises could focus on sharing your data or compromising data confidentiality or availability. Remember that the processor is a system within itself, so an attack on this system essentially compromises all output.

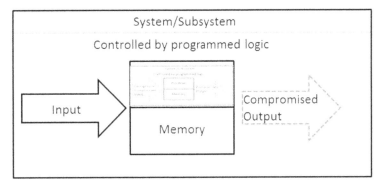

Source: Ervin Frenzel

There are of course other types of attacks that can compromise a system, so many in fact that they could not be listed inside of a chapter of a book. One recent type of attack now involves attacking the video subsystem.[2] Now the good news, manufacturers often place updated information on their websites that directly affects your systems—this can be downloaded and your systems can be updated to reduce vulnerabilities at the hardware system levels. If the manufacturer does not disclose vulnerabilities, don't give up hope. Other locations provide insight into vulnerabilities, such as commoncriteriaportal.org or other evaluation websites.

Good vulnerability scanning software will often verify that known hardware vulnerabilities have been addressed. The software will include this as part of a consolidated vulnerability report. If you choose to place vulnerability scanning software/capability inside of your network—do your homework and identify what you actually need. Some business/legal requirements may dictate the ability to detect changes within seconds of occurrence while other organizational legal requirements may not require immediate detection depending upon the system criticality. Investigative

---

2. Recent attacks at the video subsystem level are almost completely invisible to modern anti-virus programs, tell-tale signs might be the computer system sending information through covert channels at off-peak hours. Of course sending data through covert channels might be a tell-tale sign of almost any compromised system.

time should be spent determining the requirements for scanning before research is done into what type of scanning software should be obtained, this should include what additional information can be added to the overall risk determination/analysis for the organization.

SOFTWARE VULNERABILITIES

We have spent quite a bit of time talking about hardware, but a system needs some form of logic to control it. This is where software comes in; to understand how to protect software we must first understand how we build software. There is a process used that addresses almost all of these needs. There are many different methods or frameworks to identify software requirements, and most of these start with a customer/end user identifying what they want to accomplish. The programmer is not normally the individual who helps to identify requirements, normally it will be a program manager or an expert who deals with customer expectations and is capable of translating the desires into attainable goals. The programmer will not normally be able to translate the requirements as a programmer is used to thinking in the programming logic methodologies. Normally the requirements phase is the most difficult phase, after all there is now an individual in-between the end user requesting the software and the person who will be designing it—a misunderstanding between any two parties will lead to an incorrectly designed product. I see this all the time, particularly when people of multiple cultures and languages come together to attempt to produce a product.

Software design normally follows the requirements phase. Developers, designers, and programmers are now involved. This is where they find out if the program manager has over promised, failed to gather enough information, or has gathered the requirements that will distinguish it from other programs. This process may go back and forth between the program manager, customer, and the programmers until there is a clarified vision for the programmers to work with. The program manager needs to pay particular attention to ensure that the customer requirements are met and that everything is documented. It is equally important that the customer acknowledge that the design meets their expectation and signs off on the design itself. This is a common thread in the Scott Adams cartoon, *Dilbert*.

VULNERABILITIES
Weaknesses or gaps in a security program that can be exploited by threats to gain unauthorized access to an asset or assets.

Now we build the program. This is where security **vulnerabilities** really begin to show themselves. Programmers may identify that they have already completed parts of the program, outside of this particular program. This is commonly referred to as using a programming library. The weakness with this strategy is that a security issue stays a security issue, unless it is specifically corrected. Worse, if a programmer is used to building logic in a certain manner, the manner in which the programmer programs may actually create security vulnerabilities. This last group is actually harder to protect against, as it is waiting to be discovered and may become a part of a programming library further down the road. The programming library is a mainstay for programmers; after all, copy the work that you or others have already completed, save the time for development, programming, and not having to retest the software. Economically it makes sense, saves development time and money. Sounds great right? "Maybe" is the best answer we can provide.

Fundamentally we need to understand the mentality of a programmer. Programmers build programs to automate a function and save time and resources so that things can happen—generally to increase a capability. They do not program to limit capability (normally). In essence they are creators, and this is why management personnel with a vision will contact them to make things happen. This mentality while extremely creative does not normally address security, so a security person should be consulted during the creative process to ensure the program is both creative and secure.

Once the program has been built, it has to be tested. Not just any testing but it needs to be verified that it meets the customer requirements and it has to be verified that it meets security requirements. Any failures at this point need to be addressed IMMEDIATELY. My advice is that the software is not presented to the end user who set the requirements until these issues are resolved. Testing should not be the first time that security is addressed, but sadly, many times it is. Properly done, the requirements phase could address some basic security functionality—in essence security by design.

Now the end user has to accept the software, provided there has not been any scope creep from what the end user stated earlier (and signed off on with the program manager). This is where the end user can be a pain, after all this is the point where the customer expectation meets the programmer's delivery. If the programmer really understood the requirements, then the program should be fairly close—it might even be dead on, but the end user has to say it is good to go or at least acceptable. The system may need to be customized to adapt to changes to the working environment that have occurred since the program was started.

After testing, the software is generally considered to be certified to function under certain conditions, but it is still not complete. The system must now be accredited under the corporate conditions where it will be employed. This is done by management and can be part of the acceptance of the program.

Once the system has been accepted it is now employed. The programmer's job is still not done, there will be a need for updates, upgrades as needed by the end corporation, training, and ensuring the end users can use the program. What about intellectual licensing and copyrights? That should have been worked out before moving forward. Of course all programs must come to an end and when they do, they must be properly decommissioned. The process that has been discussed is often referred to as "cradle to grave."

Let's recap—keep in mind this is a very high level overview and different methodologies may have more or fewer steps than listed below:

▶ Initiate the project

▶ Identify the requirements

▶ Software design

▶ Software build

▶ Testing

▶ Customer acceptance

▶ Software deployment

▶ Maintenance

▶ Disposal

VULNERABILITY SCANNING

So how will you know if a system fails a vulnerability scan or even what is considered vulnerability? Well first we have seen how software is built, but now we introduce the concept of testing certain applications and pieces of software. During this process, we identify software as it is stored in a software library, we test this software in a very methodical process. If vulnerabilities are found they are noted and entered into a database. There are naming conventions to describe specific types of vulnerabilities for easy reference later.[3]

---

3. Sites such as http://cve.mitre.org/ have listings showing all known vulnerabilities. Sites such as mitre have large databases which can be downloaded and searched.

Now that we understand the general process that is used to develop software we might see some flaws in the system. First of all, the end user doesn't normally see the value of security so the requirements may be missing security factors, normally users are looking for functionality not security. To verify a system is secure, testing should be performed at regular intervals. Not every piece of software has to be scanned every moment of every day, but systems should be scanned at regular intervals to identify improperly configured software, applications, or even hardware configurations. In truth, business policies should reflect a standard on how often and how scanning should occur. What is a vulnerability? According to NIST a vulnerability is:

> 1.) Weakness in an information system, system security procedures, internal controls, or implementation that could be exploited or triggered by a threat source. 2.) A weakness in a system, application, or network that is subject to exploitation or misuse. 3.) Weakness in an information system, system security procedures, internal controls, or implementation that could be exploited by a threat source.

There are many different scanning engines capable of scanning systems to indicate which vulnerabilities are present. In essence these different engines throw different threats against the software and determine if the software is susceptible to a particular vulnerability. A systematic approach to vulnerabilities has been developed that provides a searchable database; this searchable database provides a basis for many of these vulnerability tools. This database is neither the only source for information, nor is it comprehensive as many individual vulnerabilities have yet to be discovered. Other vulnerabilities may be known but not disclosed, these vulnerabilities are known as "zero day" vulnerabilities and are normally known only by an attacker (there are exceptions to this in which an organization may know in advance but not disclose a vulnerability).

PATCH MANAGEMENT AND VULNERABILITY REMEDIATION

New vulnerabilities are discovered as software interacts with systems, including hardware and newer software. Oddly a security patch for one piece of software can actually cause vulnerabilities or failures in other software, so knowing what you have for software is very important. Many larger organizations have teams that have the sole responsibility of identifying how different software patches will interact with the individual systems and the entire system for the organization. Other organizations have individual application teams responsible for ensuring that their software remains compliant (sometimes it is not a very sound process as testing often becomes redundant and overly time-consuming).

PATCH MANAGEMENT
Planning the cycle of security updates to software.

An important concept is **patch management**. Plan your patching cycle because many software organizations have announced patch cycles. Your organization should take the time to learn the software support cycles that are available; most software vendors normally make patches publicly available at little or no cost. Being a student of your system(s) will pay great dividends in the long run. More importantly ensuring that your trusted organizations also are students of their own systems will yield dividends that not even one of your organizations could comprehend initially.

Now for the legal aspect, many compliance requirements will dictate that you are not only a student of your own systems but also that your aligned organizations are aware of your systems and you of theirs. In the HIPAA and PCI worlds, as well as others, this is something that audits will check for. Audit teams should look for policies that support this and penetration test teams will normally test to make sure that this is more than just a paperwork drill.

Remember, a penetration tester should identify anything that they change, and they should identify it to the appropriate persons. The "appropriate" persons should not only have the authority to make the changes but should also have the primary responsibility to remediate the situation. If the person is lacking in either then the organization may actually be worse off than before the test. This does not mean the person needs to be the technician who makes the changes, but the technicians should somehow be responsible to this supervisor. Remember remediating is a team effort, technicians should not only be experienced but be willing to continue their education. A team member who is isolated is ineffective, and worse, because a lack of timely information will become a hindrance to effective issue resolution. If a team member tries to place themselves above their peers, at the cost of their teammates, they should not be on this team and managers/supervisors should take all actions to remove elements that will become destructive to the remediation team no matter how good the technician. This may be as simple as taking time for team building to occur and encouraging team building exercises or as complex as removing team members who become destructive to the ability to remediate vulnerabilities.

In the case of trusted organizations, time should be spent making sure that trust between the persons who work with these vulnerabilities is built and maintained. This shouldn't be anything new though, remember a little bit of competition is good, squashing team members to favor a single team member or appease an ego is destructive and will eventually destroy the entire team thus affecting the overall organization and failing to remediate anything.

CONCLUSION

This is one of the most important chapters in this book. Knowing how to communicate between management and software and hardware designers is essential to ensuring the end product is not only what was originally conceived, but is safe and secure. Having a plan in place that addresses these points is essential to success when it comes to hardware and software.

For an organization to properly plan a defense of its systems, it must first understand the threats that it faces. Every hardware and software system/subsystem has an attack footprint that must be addressed but only after it has been uncovered. **Software vulnerabilities** are often discovered through vulnerability scanning and can be remediated through patch management and proper managerial techniques.

Don't just hire any penetration tester. When you determine that external penetration testing is appropriate, be certain to specify clearly what is to be tested, not to be tested, and how vulnerabilities are to be addressed. This is essential to ensuring the test is not only performed with quality, but meets the contractual and legal requirements appropriate for your organization and country. When working with organizations that span multiple countries—the penetration testing protocol must ensure that all the legal requirements of each country involved must be met.

Understanding the team aspects of remediation teams is critical to full remediation of the systems within an organization. Trusted networks must be treated as a threat vector the same as internal network assets. A network is only as strong as its weakest link whether that is hardware, software, or human.

QUESTIONS FOR FURTHER CONSIDERATION

1. Communicate with your agency/organization IT department and determine when the last external audit of your computer systems was conducted. Is this audit process conducted on a regular basis? Should it be?

2. If a penetration tester was to identify a vulnerability in one of your computer systems how would you approach the issue and whom would you inform?

3. Looking at all of the current systems used in your agency/organization, try to determine how many different software programs are currently running on your system. Try to determine how many computer

SOFTWARE VULNERABILITIES
The inherent and intentional or unintentional gaps in programing that allow outside programs to utilize or corrupt a system.

components are attached and interact with your system. Can you find places where efficiency can be implemented and vulnerability reduced?

REFERENCES

Adams, Scott. *Dilbert*. http://dilbert.com.

Merriam-Webster. (n.d.). *Merriam-Webster Online*. Computer [Def. 2, Full definition]. http://merriam-webster.com/dictionary/citation.

NIST Special Publication (SP) 800-64, Revision 2, *Security Considerations in the System Development Life Cycle*.

NISTIR 7298 Revision 2, Glossary of Key Information Security Terms. 2013. Threat [Full Definition]. http://nvlpubs.nist.gov/nistpubs/ir/2013/NIST.IR.7298r2.pdf.

NISTIR 7298 Revision 2, Glossary of Key Information Security Terms. 2013. Vulnerability [Full Definition]. http://nvlpubs.nist.gov/nistpubs/ir/2013/NIST.IR.7298r2.pdf.

CHAPTER 8

EXAMINING VULNERABILITY: THE PROBLEM WITH INTERNET PROVIDERS AND E-MAIL

KEY WORDS

Browser History	ISP	SPAM
Fraud	Phishing	Spear-Phishing
Full Header	Ransomware	Spoofing
IP Address		

INTRODUCTION

The Internet offers a tremendous resource for those wanting to share information or conduct business globally. You can communicate with anybody anywhere at any time. You can even e-mail the astronauts on the International Space Station. What you can do, so can a machine or algorithm or botnet. So, just because an e-mail comes from somebody or a company that you trust doesn't mean that the e-mail is real or safe. Determining that is up to you. You might consider using digital signatures and encryption between key personnel to make sure that e-mails cannot be spoofed— while this will not completely eliminate the threat it will reduce it. Be creative, create a system to verify e-mails and enforce it. It may include a challenge and response for "C" level officers who request transfers of money via e-mail. There are many creative solutions to verifying e-mails and your organization should investigate these solutions or create some

of their own. This could simply be the first of many layers required to defend your systems. Remember, e-mails are something that you must investigate if they are questionable.

Even if you install anti-spam software on your system, you will still be subject to any number of e-mail attacks daily. E-mail can be **SPAM/Spoofing**, **phishing**, **fraud**, **ransomware**, and all the other types of criminal behavior previously specified. Determining if something is real depends on how you look at the object received and the level of training you incorporate into your organization. How you recognize and deal with these daily e-mail attacks is up to you.

SPAM
Unsolicited bulk e-mail.

SPOOFING
The dissemination of e-mail which is forged to appear as though it was sent by someone other than the actual source.

PHISHING
Forged or faked electronic documents intended to acquire personal information to commit another Internet crime.

FRAUD
The act of using a computer to take or alter electronic data, or to gain unlawful use of a computer or system.

RANSOMWARE
Malicious software inadvertently downloaded to a computer that subsequently locks the computer screen until an acceptable pass code is entered, usually after some sort of money transfer.

UNDER ATTACK

E-mail forgery is common and easy to do. The issue is that we (the recipient) don't always figure out that what we are looking at is a problem e-mail until AFTER we have mistakenly clicked on a link that takes us to a video, or downloads a virus or key logger, or installs ransomware on the computer and locks us out of our own system until we pay. This is where modern technology moves from being beneficial to being problematic and criminal.

Each of the following e-mails consist of a variety of types of attacks. You can see a Connection-based Attack, SPAM, Phishing, and E-mail Viruses. All of these appeared on the author's own system in the fall of 2016 and these are just a couple of over forty-five junk e-mails that were routed to our ISP mail client in a five-day period of time.

Let's examine a SPAM/SPOOF e-mail in one of the author's own accounts. We've modified the actual e-mail address of the author in these images but otherwise all the images are original. As you can see in Figure 8.1, the e-mail supposedly came from the author and was sent to the author. This is spoofing and that it is asking for information is phishing. Two types of attack in a single e-mail.

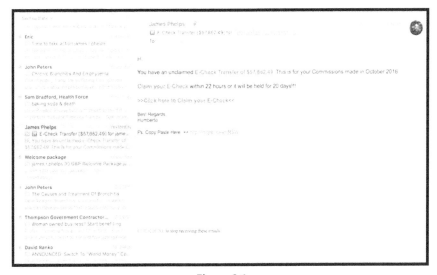

Figure 8.1

You've probably seen something that looks like this before. When we examine some of the links in this e-mail here is what we see:

Figure 8.2

Figure 8.3

Figure 8.4

While we wonder what is on these videos—we're not dumb enough to open them to find out. Doing so would expose our computers to all sorts of attacks including the installation of software that might be hazardous.

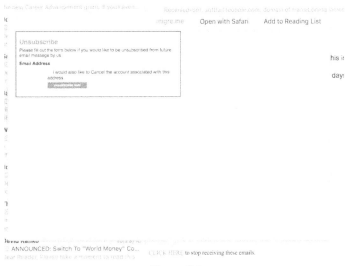

Figure 8.5

In Figure 8.5 we see what information is included in the Unsubscribe link at the bottom of the e-mail. **NEVER** fill one of these out unless you know the real sender and trust them with your information. All you are doing when you complete one of these blocks is identifying that the e-mail address the message was sent to is in fact a valid and actively used address. The program that collects this information will then sell it to other spammers and you will suddenly see a major increase in your junk traffic.

One of the ways to look at who an e-mail is actually from is to look at the **full header**. Your e-mail program should provide you an option that allows this. Figure 8.6 is the full header information for the e-mail in Figure 8.1:

FULL HEADER

In e-mail messages, full headers contain the addresses of all the computer systems that have relayed a message in-between you and the message's sender.

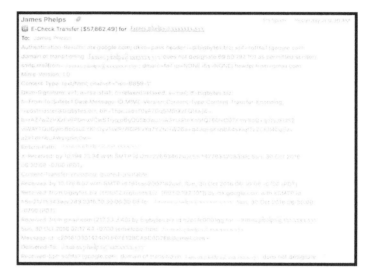

Figure 8.6

Through this information you can backtrack each and every system that sent the e-mail from originator to your inbox. Here is another full header from another SPAM e-mail. In this case the full header wouldn't actually appear on a single screen, so the very last line is cut off in this image.

Figure 8.7

SPEAR-PHISHING
The fraudulent practice of sending e-mails ostensibly from a known or trusted sender in order to induce targeted individuals to reveal confidential information.

Here is another e-mail showing what is called a **spear-phishing** attack. The e-mail claims to be from USAA, an insurance and banking company associated with current and former members of the US military and their dependents. USAA is a highly reputable company and won't ask for their clients to provide any kind of personal or account information via e-mail.

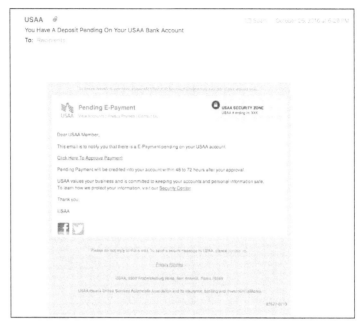

Figure 8.8

Note that the e-mail address looks like it comes from USAA. Yet, as you can see in Figure 8.9, the e-mail doesn't really come from USAA:

Figure 8.9

Here is the full header information.

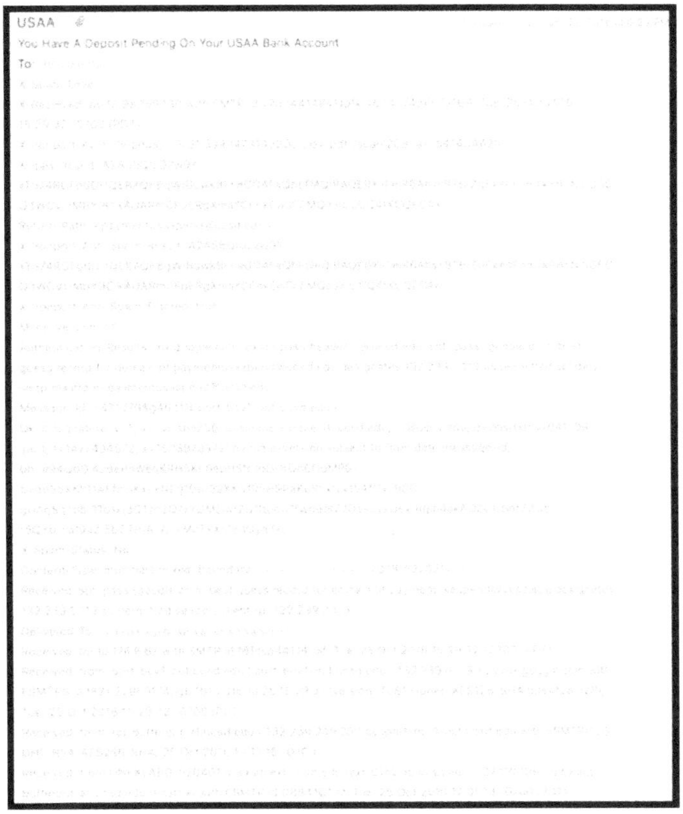

Figure 8.10

IP ADDRESSES
The specific and unique numbers assigned to computers.

If we look at the USAA e-mail in Figure 8.9 and Figure 8.10 we see that the original **IP address** is 132.239.0.119 and is indicated as originating from a computer at the University of California San Diego. We wonder if UCSD knows that one of their computers is sending batches of e-mail attacks? A quick Google search on the IP offers the following possible results:

Figure 8.11

As we've said before, there are methods of establishing firewalls and other protective screens, including blacklists and whitelists that will help our computer system to identify and filter these sorts of scams and attacks. How our agency configures these is up to us and our IT departments.

▶ Every computer should have multiple firewall systems.

▶ Every computer should have Ad Blocker Programs.

▶ Every computer should have an updated Whitelist and Blacklist and should offer a means to readily mark incoming communications as SPAM or Junk that can be filtered automatically for all subsequent items originating from the same place or sender.

On our personal computers, we also maintain multiple means of protection. Even if you use a Mac you need protection. This author uses MacKeeper—an externally provided screen and clean program that includes 24/7/365 live help and cleaning of my computer at any time and where ever we may be in the world. This sort of service is expensive. In fact, it can be pretty expensive. However, the same service also covers my other

Mac products like my iPhone, and even a stand-alone PC I use only for GIS and SPSS work. So, sometimes having this type of protection is worth the expense, particularly if you are dependent upon your computers for your livelihood.

DETERMINING THE ORIGIN AND ROUTERS

Way back in Chapter 1 we listed all the IP addresses that processed the e-mail containing the Chapter 1 Draft file between the authors. Here they are again:

    104.47.42.119
    25.173.146.132
    10.202.177.6
    10.176.6.67
    10.168.238.13
    10.168.238.15
    15.1.734.8
    15.01.0734.014

Let's take a look at these IP addresses from a different perspective and determine where that e-mail went between the two author's computers. Using www.iploaction.net we can see that:

104.47.42.119	Microsoft Corporation, San Jose, California
25.173.146.132	UK Ministry of Defence, London, England
10.202.177.6	Emirates Integrated Telecommunications Company (EITC), Dubai, UAE
10.176.6.67	EITC, Dubai, UAE
10.168.238.13	EITC, Dubai, UAE
10.168.238.15	EITC, Dubai, UAE
15.1.734.8	EICT, International City, Dubai, UAE
15.01.0734.014	EICT, International City, Dubai, UAE

Using another program, whois.arin.net, we can find out who owns these IP addresses. The results for the first one on the list, 104.47.42.119, are found in Figures 8.12–8.16 and are exactly what we would expect from a server/router operated by the Microsoft Corporation.

You searched for: **104.47.42.119**

Network	
Net Range	104.40.0.0 - 104.47.255.255
CIDR	104.40.0.0/13
Name	MSFT
Handle	NET-104-40-0-0-1
Parent	NET104 (NET-104-0-0-0-0)
Net Type	Direct Assignment
Origin AS	
Organization	Microsoft Corporation (MSFT)
Registration Date	2014-05-07
Last Updated	2014-05-07
Comments	
RESTful Link	https://whois.arin.net/rest/net/NET-104-40-0-0-1
See Also	Related organization's POC records.
See Also	Related delegations.

Figure 8.12

Organization	
Name	Microsoft Corporation
Handle	MSFT
Street	One Microsoft Way
City	Redmond
State/Province	WA
Postal Code	98052
Country	US
Registration Date	1998-07-10
Last Updated	2016-06-30
Comments	To report suspected security issues specific to traffic emanating from Microsoft online services, including the distribution of malicious content or other illicit or illegal material through a Microsoft online service, please submit reports to: * https://cert.microsoft.com.
	For SPAM and other abuse issues, such as Microsoft Accounts, please contact: * abuse@microsoft.com.
	To report security vulnerabilities in Microsoft products and services, please contact: * secure@microsoft.com.
	For legal and law enforcement-related requests, please contact: * msndcc@microsoft.com
	For routing, peering or DNS issues, please contact: * IOC@microsoft.com
RESTful Link	https://whois.arin.net/rest/org/MSFT

Function	Point of Contact
Abuse	MAC74-ARIN (MAC74-ARIN)
Tech	MRPD-ARIN (MRPD-ARIN)
Admin	QUAMA-ARIN (QUAMA-ARIN)

Figure 8.13

Figure 8.14

Figure 8.15

Point of Contact	
Name	Quamara , Divya
Handle	QUAMA-ARIN
Company	Microsoft
Street	One Microsoft Way
City	Redmond
State/Province	WA
Postal Code	98052
Country	US
Registration Date	2015-09-25
Last Updated	2016-05-25
Comments	
Phone	+1-425-706-2751 (Office)
Email	diquamar@microsoft.com
RESTful Link	https://whois.arin.net/rest/poc/QUAMA-ARIN

Figure 8.16

When we check the owner of the second IP address, 25.173.146.132, the one that is listed as being at the UK Ministry of Defence, London, England, we find that it doesn't seem to be operated by that agency. Instead, this IP address is an early IP registration from 1985!! And while located in London, as you can see in Figures 8.17 and 8.18, is operated by a legacy host organization known as 'Reseaux IP Europeens Network Coordination Centre - RIPE NCC' operating out of Amsterdam.

You searched for 25.173.146.132

Network	
Net Range	25.0.0.0 - 25.255.255.255
CIDR	25.0.0.0/8
Name	RIPE-ERX-25
Handle	NET-25-0-0-0-1
Parent	
Net Type	Early Registrations, Maintained by RIPE NCC
Origin AS	
Organization	RIPE Network Coordination Centre (RIPE)
Registration Date	1985-01-28
Last Updated	2013-01-14
Comments	These addresses have been further assigned to users in the RIPE NCC region. Contact information can be found in the RIPE database at https://www.ripe.net/whois
RESTful Link	https://whois.arin.net/rest/net/NET-25-0-0-0-1
See Also	Related organization's POC records.
See Also	Resource links.
See Also	Related delegations.

Figure 8.17

Figure 8.18

Following this trail one step further, we go to the RIPE.net website and enter the IP address again. This time it tells us this **IS STILL** an IP address recorded and operated by the UK Ministry of Defence (Figure 8.19). It even gives us the name and telephone number of the person at the UK Ministry of Defence that is responsible for this device (Figure 8.20). As you can see in Figure 8.20, the contact information was updated as recently as 22 November 2016.

Figure 8.19

```
person:          Mathew Newton                          Login to update ▤
address:         Network Technical Authority
address:         UK Ministry of Defence
phone:           +44 (0)30 677 00816
e-mail:          mathew.newton643@mod.gov.uk
abuse-mailbox:   hostmaster@mod.uk
notify:          mathew.newton643@mod.gov.uk
nic-hdl:         MN1861-RIPE
created:         2005-03-18T10:42:04Z
last-modified:   2016-11-22T20:15:10Z
source:          RIPE
mnt-by:          UK-MOD-MNT
```

Figure 8.20

So now we have some idea of how an e-mail got from one place in the US to another place in the UAE. The whole process has a number of ways it can be traced and there are a lot of programs out there that will allow you to reverse trace communications from point to point. Getting into that process isn't our intent and is fundamentally the function of those who work in the IT department. Let's leave those processes to them.

ISP
Internet Service Provider.

BROWSER HISTORY
The list of web pages a user has visited recently—and associated data such as page title and time of visit—which is recorded by web browser software as standard for a certain period of time.

WHAT ABOUT THE ISP?

While e-mail is problematic from a number of security reasons, the Internet and those that provide service access to it are also problematic. Consider, for example, your web **browser history.**

OK—so what is web browser history? Simply said, every time you look at or visit a web page or conduct a search for information on the Internet a record of that search or viewing is retained by the Internet service provider and your search engine. This is a complete list of the web pages the user has recently visited as well as the associated data such as the page title and time of visit. Where can you find this information? On your computer itself, in the browser tool bar. On the server that services your computer if you are using a work system or home network and on the search engine website itself. For example, in Figure 8.21 we see the history for a computer that uses the Apple browser, Safari. Nothing abnormal or unusual here . . .

Figure 8.21

So, if you want to know what that employee has been looking at instead of working on the assigned project, there is a way to recover that information from the system records. While they might be able to clear their history from the computer itself, they won't be able to erase history from the system servers. This is one way people who search pornography websites at work are frequently caught. Even though they thought they cleared the record, and even cleared the search engine record on the Internet, the system between the two will still have a record that can't be eliminated without administrator access.

If you are interested in what your child or spouse is looking at on the web—in all likelihood they haven't erased their history in some time. It might be interesting if you checked sometime. Figure 8.22 shows a partial Safari Browser history for the MacBook used to write this chapter. Note that there are thirty-eight items from this day alone. Now consider Figure 8.23—the browser history goes all the way back to 1 December

2015!!! Makes you sort of wonder what I was looking at back then. I checked and you can see the results in Figure 8.24. I sure am glad I wasn't looking at pornography or terrorist sites back then. That would be embarrassing for the publisher and my co-author.

Figure 8.22

Figure 8.23

Figure 8.24

By the way – I just pressed that (Clear History) button at the top right side of the page . . .

CONCLUSION

In looking at the issues of e-mail and ISPs we can see there are a lot of vulnerabilities we are exposed to on a daily basis. Much of these threat processes are referred to as Social Engineering. In dealing with these threats the fundamental problem isn't our computer security or the firewall or the spam blocker. The basic problem for all these threats is the people themselves. We can train, educate, remind, and even punish those that break cybersecurity protocol. Unfortunately, that won't fix the problems their actions cause. You only have to be hit with ransomware once to feel the real pain your agency is exposed to by these vulnerabilities. You only have to get one really nasty worm injected into your system to find that your data has been destroyed from within. In the end, the most basic yet important protection is going to be the computer operator.

QUESTIONS FOR FURTHER CONSIDERATION

1. How can you determine where your computer has surfed to?

2. Describe the route taken from your computer to www.google.com by using a command prompt and then typing "tracert www.google.com." What can you learn from the steps/routers in-between?

3. Release and renew your IP address (command prompt, then type "ipconfig /release" followed by typing "ipconfig /renew"). Now repeat the steps in the last question. Did the route or the final IP address for Google change? If so, why did it happen?

4. Identify some methods of ensuring e-mail that you have received is safe, and how can you confirm the authorship of these e-mails?

REFERENCES

IP Location. 2016. Available at: https://www.iplocation.net.

Reseaux IP Europeens (RIPE) Network Coordination Centre. 2016. https://www.ripe.net.

SANS™ Institute. 2016. http://www.sans.org.

Social Engineer, Inc. 2016. http://www.social-engineer.org.

CHAPTER 9

THE WORLD WIDE WEB: PUBLIC, DARK, AND TOR

KEY WORDS

CA/Browser Forum	ICANN	RFID
Dark Web	Internet of Things	Tor
Deep Web	Onion Router	World Wide Web
FCC	Public Web	

ORIGINS OF THE PUBLIC WEB

WORLD WIDE WEB
An interconnected web of servers that simply switch packets of information around the globe.

We are in a golden age of communication and information access, thanks to the success of the **World Wide Web** and the foundation of the globally-connected Internet. To understand what the WWW is, we first should take a trip back into the past. Much of what we consider the public web today can be attributed to three developments.

In 1969 the Department of Defense funds ARPANET, a packet-switching network for use by scientists and the military. This originally began when the Advanced Research Projects Agency contacted Bold, Beranek, and Newman (BBN) Technologies of Cambridge, Mass., in 1968 to build the first routers. One year later, the Advanced Research Projects Agency Network (ARPANET) became operational.

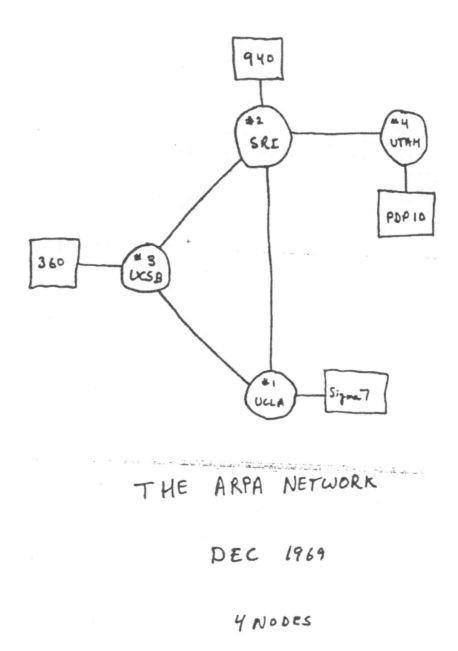

Figure 9.1   A sketch of the ARPANET in December 1969. The nodes at UCLA and the Stanford Research Institute (SRI) are among those depicted. From *50 Years of Bridging the Gap,* "DARPA and the Internet Revolution" by Mitch Waldrop, DARPA, United States Department of Defense.

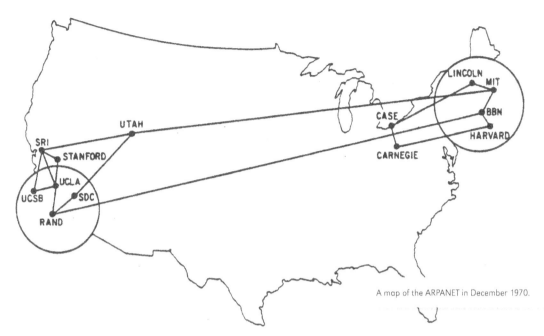

Figure 9.2   A map of ARPANET in 1970. From *50 Years of Bridging the Gap,* "DARPA and the Internet Revolution" by Mitch Waldrop, DARPA, United States Department of Defense.

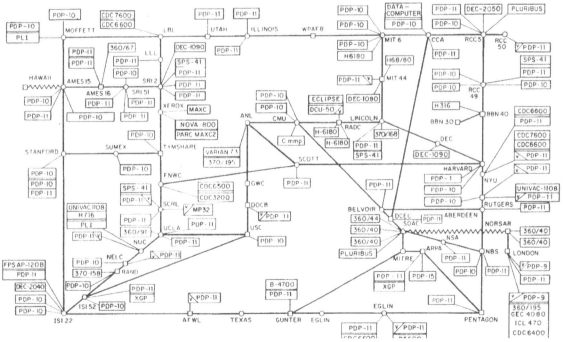

Figure 9.3   By the late 1970s the concept of a communications network where scientists and the military could share information between locations had taken full form. From *50 Years of Bridging the Gap,* "DARPA and the Internet Revolution" by Mitch Waldrop, DARPA, United States Department of Defense.

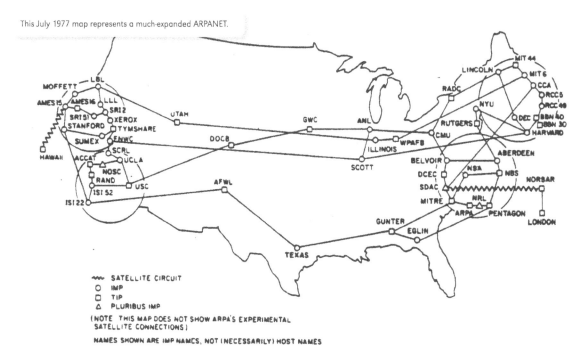

This July 1977 map represents a much-expanded ARPANET.

Figure 9.4   By the late 1970s the expanse of ARPANET had broken the bounds of the continental United States and reached Hawaii and London via satellite links. From *50 Years of Bridging the Gap*, "DARPA and the Internet Revolution" by Mitch Waldrop, DARPA, United States Department of Defense.

In 1974 Robert Kahn published a paper entitled, "A Protocol for Packet Network Interconnection" that described a network architecture using Transmission Control Protocol/Internet Protocol (TCP/IP) that held the whole thing together. Kahn asked Vincent Cerf of Stanford University to collaborate on a project to develop this new protocol for sending packets of data across ARPANET. By March 1982 the Department of Defense felt the whole ARPANET concept was reliable and secure enough to make TCP/IP the standard for all military computer networking. On January 1, 1983, ARPANET switched itself over to TCP/IP and the Internet as we know it was born.

With ARPANET's evolution into the modern "Internet" commercial entities are given access and the first .COM domain is registered in 1985 (symbolics.com). In March 1989 Tim Berners-Lee, a scientist at CERN, proposed the creation of a World Wide Web using hypertext. This undated proposal was later added a May 1990 date. The purpose was to find lost packets of information that CERN couldn't find.

Berners-Lee's proposal was generated in RTF by MSWord in 1998 and is available at: https://www.w3.org/History/1989/proposal-msw.html.

In 1993 a team working at the National Center for Supercomputing Applications (NCSA), led by Marc Andreeson, publishes the Mosaic web browser. Later this is licensed by Microsoft for Internet Explorer, and serves as the basis for Netscape Navigator, and later, Mozilla Firefox. What used to be limited to a select number of scientists, is now open to the globe, where with a few dollars, anyone can register a domain name and publish a website. Getting access to the Internet and viewing a webpage is even easier, as nearly half of the globe's population will have access by the end of 2016.

Today, anyone with a smartphone or laptop can access the web, but this wasn't always so easy. The first public users of the web required bulky and expensive computer setups using complicated software, which required special skills to set up and maintain. This provided a high barrier for entry, and in effect limited the amount of crime that was perpetrated over the Internet. Consequently, the high-profile incidents from the eighties and nineties can be attributed to specialized hackers targeting a handful of companies, such as the Digital Equipment Corporation and Pacific Bell hacks perpetrated by black hat hacker Kevin Mitnick. Federal prosecutors claimed that Mitnick could "start a nuclear war by whistling into a pay phone," which became the basis for the iconic 1983 Matthew Broderick hacking film, *War Games*.

© ra2studio/Shutterstock.com

HOW IT IS USED TODAY

Over the last twenty years there has been a sea-change in technology, as consumers have access to an amazing range of inexpensive and sophisticated devices. Consumers have benefited from advances in manufacturing, electronic sensors, and evolving mobile phone networks (T-Mobile currently offers the fastest mobile broadband in the US at 16Mbps, enough to download a DVD wirelessly to your smartphone in thirty-seven minutes), culminating in the ever-evolving smartphone options we have today, concentrated in two dominant groups: Apple iPhones and Google Android-based smartphones. These useful devices have become the most popular way to surf the web today.

Businesses have successfully capitalized on the public's interest in the web by continually developing new markets (e-commerce, social networking, ride-sharing, online video) and producing devices that are easier to use.

This popularity can be measured in the number of people with access to the web, which is nearly half the globe's population, and 80 percent of those living in developed countries.

INTERNET OF THINGS
Describes a recent trend to incorporate technology into nearly every aspect of our physical world.

RFID
Radio frequency identification chips.

The **Internet of Things** describes a recent trend to incorporate technology into nearly every aspect of our physical world, from car tires to televisions, and even toilets. This term was coined in 1999 by Kevin Ashton as widespread use of **radio frequency identification chips (RFID)** began to take hold, and today we can imagine a home completely filled with Internet-connected devices, providing a myriad of benefits. Thanks to these new devices and the Internet, you can remotely monitor your home through inexpensive security cameras, remotely unlock your front door, and control the temperature. You can also bring down entire network communication systems as was done on 20 October 2016 when the domain host Dyn was brought to a halt by a DDOS attack conducted by hacked "Internet of Things" comprised of everything from toasters and televisions to thermostats. Due to the re-use of certain poorly-designed components, a security defect can find its way into dozens of products, often with no way for a manufacturer to correct after the product is sold. One such component made by Xiongmai is responsible for the largest DDoS (distributed denial of service) attack to date at over 600 Gbps. Through brute force hacking or reverse engineering, hackers managed to guess the default password used for IoT devices like security cameras and DVRs, and repurposed them as DDoS bots. When grouped together, these form large armies that can deliver devastating attacks, known as "Internet Cannons." Owners of these compromised devices have little way of knowing they are involved.

In the race to develop new devices, some companies have cut corners, and neglected to introduce even basic security. Consider the example of the "Smart" toilet, My Satis Bluetooth-connected toilet. The Bluetooth password of "0000" is hardcoded into the $6,000 device, allowing any neighbor to remotely flush the toilet.

HOW THE INTERNET IS MANAGED AND POLICED

The seemingly simple act of visiting a website can involve dozens of different companies, from the web browser and device you're using, your Internet Service Provider connection, the Domain Name System registries, Tier 1 providers maintaining the backbone of the Internet, website hosting companies and their data centers, advertising networks, secure certificate providers, and finally to the oftentimes complex software which serves up a web page showing photos of kittens. Due to the number of entities involved, as well as the global nature of the web, there are few organizations that manage the Internet, and those that do focus on technical elements:

ICANN
The Internet Corporation for Assigned Names and Numbers, a nonprofit organization that primarily maintains the root DNS system.

▶ **ICANN**—The Internet Corporation for Assigned Names and Numbers, a nonprofit organization that primarily maintains the root DNS system. This ensures that requests for apple.com or google.com are correctly routed to the servers owned by the companies Apple and Google, and not mis-routed to a criminal's faked website. Prior to 30 September 2016, the US Department of Commerce held ultimate responsibility for managing the root DNS configuration, but this is no longer the case, and control of the Internet's naming system is now an independent multi-stakeholder process.

CA/BROWSER FORUM
The Certification Authority Browser Forum, a group comprised of the leading browser and Certification Authority companies.

▶ **CA/Browser Forum**—The Certification Authority Browser Forum, a group comprised of the leading browser and Certification Authority companies, issues guidance concerning the issuance and handling of X.509 certificates, commonly used to support SSL and HTTPS websites.

> Recommendation ITU-T X.509 | ISO/IEC 9594-8 defines frameworks for public-key infrastructure (PKI) and privilege management infrastructure (PMI). It introduces the basic concept of asymmetric cryptographic techniques. It specifies the following data types: public-key certificate, attribute certificate, certificate revocation list (CRL) and attribute certificate revocation list (ACRL). It also defines several certificates and CRL extensions, and it defines directory schema information allowing PKI and PMI related data to be stored in a directory. In addition, it defines entity types, such as certification authority (CA), attribute authority (AA), relying party, privilege verifier, trust broker and trust anchor. It specifies the principles for certificate validation, validation path, certificate policy, etc. It includes a specification for authorization validation lists that allow for fast validation and restrictions on communications. It includes protocols necessary for maintaining authorization validation lists and a protocol for accessing a trust broker. (http://www.itu.int)

FCC
Federal Communications Commission, which oversees telecommunications in the United States.

▶ The **FCC**—The Federal Communications Commission, which oversees telecommunications in the United States, issued "The Open Internet Order" in 2015 which provides three rules for ISPs: "(1) no blocking; (2) no unreasonable discrimination; and (3) transparency" (FCC 15-24).

US President Barack Obama has warned of the possibility that the Internet could become like the "Wild, Wild West." We see that happening with the 20 October 2016 DDOS attack on Dyn and the hacking of the Democrat National Committee and the subsequent release of e-mail communications indicative of internal manipulation of the 2016 Democrat primary process. It may no longer be a possibility, but a fact that the world has entered a "Wild, Wild West" version of communications.

THE INTERNET POLICE

Maintaining law and order on the public web is extremely difficult. The same ease which anyone can find anything they want on the Internet can be used by criminals to commit a number of crimes: harassment, digital theft, vandalism, and terrorism. Getting hacked on the Internet is a matter of when, and not if, and the current mindset for businesses favors detection as well as classic prevention techniques like antivirus and firewalls. Every company that makes up the Forbes 500 list has been hacked at some point. One compounding problem that society has had to deal with is "law lag," as technology continues to advance faster than rules and regulations can be applied.

If you deposit your life savings of $250,000 with a bank, but they get robbed, your savings are generally protected by FDIC insurance. The same protections do not apply if you decide to put your savings into a Bitcoin wallet. There are countless stories of Bitcoin banks and exchanges that have been robbed with little recourse for depositors. As a side note, banking in the US largely began in the 1780s, but it wasn't until the Great Depression of the 1930s, and the thousands of companies that went insolvent, that the FDIC (Federal Deposit Insurance Company) was created through an Act of Congress. In the US there are a number of laws specifically addressing crime on the Internet:

▶ Children's Internet Protection Act (CIPA)—Introduced in 2000, this law addresses Internet safety for K–12 schools that receive public funding.

▶ Communications Decency Act (CDA)—Largely ruled unconstitutional, Section 230 still applies, protecting ISPs from liabilities involved in transmitting offensive content if they are found to act in good faith.

▶ Digital Millennium Copyright Act (DMCA)—A 1998 law that addresses copyright infringement, and attempts to bypass copyright protection mechanisms. It also limits liabilities for ISPs to the actions of its users.

► Trading with the Enemy Act—This 1917 bill established the Office of Foreign Assets Control, which in recent years has used its authority to direct domain name registries to blacklist certain websites.

Let's say that you live in Texas and like to shop online with your favorite retailer "Bullseye." Because you're a frequent customer, you opt to store your credit card details on their system, allowing for easier and quicker shopping. If hackers from Eastern Europe were to break into Bullseye's servers, hosted in Minnesota, and then sold that information on the dark web, then there would be multiple legal jurisdictions involved, as well as multiple law enforcement agencies.

THE PUBLIC WEB

There are over one billion websites on the World Wide Web today. This milestone was first reached in September of 2014, as confirmed by NetCraft in its October 2014 Web Server Survey and first estimated and announced by Internet Live Stats (http://www.internetlivestats.com). About 75 percent of these are inactive, just claimed domain names, or similar. This still leaves millions of accessible websites on the public web, including popular sites like Facebook, Google, and YouTube.

© Twin Design/Shutterstock.com

The search engine Google currently indexes 60 trillion web pages, all catalogued and ranked to power the search results it has become known for. Indexing is the process of following a link to a page, consuming all the text and links on the page, creating rankings associated with each link based on a number of factors including a link's popularity (the first version of Google's search algorithm was called PageRank, after co-founder Larry Page). What makes search engines like Google so powerful are the vast quantities of publicly accessible data available on the Internet. Getting your web page to show up first in the Google search results has become a key goal for many businesses. There's even an industry dedicated to this called SEO (search engine optimization).

Search engines like Google are so powerful because they have access to a tremendous amount of publicly accessible websites. It's estimated that there are currently 1.4 billion unique websites on the public web today.

This does not include sites stored or cached versions of a given site for historical reference.[1] Maintaining a website requires highly skilled labor to create and maintain, such as that found in professional software developers, of which there are approximately 16 million people actively working in 2016. In addition to professionals (some of which may work in non-web fields like games and operating systems), there are countless others who maintain websites as hobbyists, or professionals in other industries that maintain websites part-time. Although there are benefits to creating a custom site from scratch, such as SEO optimization, even a complete novice can create a website using one of the popular website builder programs found online, such as Squarespace, Weebly, or Wix.

Over on the commercial side of things, some companies use advertising to fund their operating expenses, although the advent of ad blocking technology limits this somewhat. Advertising networks are the equivalent of TV commercials broadcasting in various markets and on different channels. Unfortunately, these sometimes act as an attack vector for viruses and malicious software, allowing a criminal to easily target a wide and diverse array of web users. The same ease that was programmed into software to enable marketing and advertisers to gain access to their consumer base is the same basis that an attacker will start from when they choose to attack an individual or an organization.

Media sites like the online New York Times, LexisNexis, and NFL.com have opted for paywalls, which require paid subscriptions to view full content. Several of the references used in writing this chapter required access to articles on paid subscription websites. Give some of them a try and you'll see what we mean. Particularly sites like Forbes. These paid sites are flexible in that they may allow a search engine's robot to crawl to some of the content, allowing a user to see a snippet of the content in a search engine, but requires a login to see the full contents of the page. As we review more closed types of websites, another group are membership-only forums. Some simply require public registration, while others require an invitation from an existing member.

Further down the scale, we have corporate and government networks, often called intranets. These often require the user to authenticate to an organization's security system and use an encrypted connection like a

---

1. Sites such as archive.org have cache sites which maintain a historical version of a site for a given duration; that duration may change according to the size of the website stored or how frequently the site is changed. Sites such as these can be used to view changes that have occurred and are often researched by penetration testers to learn about an organization.

VPN (virtual private network). One way to think about these networks is that data can freely go out, such as opening the website facebook.com, but inbound access from the Internet is restricted by default. Some companies install custom search engines, also known as network appliances, to provide indexed search results solely within the organization's network.

Sometimes a public website may host publicly accessible content that it doesn't necessarily want to be picked up by a search engine's crawler, and so a robots.txt file will be used to instruct the search engine which files should and should not be indexed. This is not considered to be a secure standard, as some spam and malicious bots may use the robot's configuration to go directly to links they are asked not to index.[2]

There are other networks which are completely disconnected from the Internet, such as classified military networks like the U.S. Department of Defense's SIPRNET. These have what's known as an air-gap to prevent classified data from accidentally spilling out onto the public Internet. Unfortunately, the air gap doesn't prevent the primary means of losing data—people.

DEEP WEB AND DARK WEB

The **public web** is anything on the Internet which a search engine has access to. If content is hosted on the Internet but protected by a paywall, login screen, or other type of authentication scheme, that falls into the category of the deep web. There is a third category we discuss in this chapter, and that is the subsection of the **deep web** which requires special browsers to access, the dark web. There are a few different types of **dark webs**, most of which are overlay networks that operate on the public Internet, using special software to anonymize traffic going in and out, with encryption to limit surveillance by law enforcement and intelligence agencies. The most popular of these networks is the The Onion Router (Tor) network.

PUBLIC WEB
Anything on the Internet to which a search engine has access.

DEEP WEB
Anything on the Internet which is not indexed by a search engine.

DARK WEB
A subset of the deep web, which requires special software and/or authorization to access.

---

2. This is a common practice for both mal-actors and security personnel alike.

THE ONION ROUTER (TOR)

TOR
The Onion Router, an overlay network that operates on the public web, which uses increasing layers of encryption to make end-to-end web traffic anonymous.

ONION ROUTER
An overlay network that operates on the public web, which uses increasing layers of encryption to make end-to-end web traffic anonymous.

Tor, derived from the original project name 'The Onion Router,' is an overlay network that operates on the public web, which uses increasing layers of encryption to make end-to-end web traffic anonymous. There are several benefits to using Tor as an anonymous network, one of which is the freedom to openly express information from an area that normally represses such information. The US Department of State's Bureau of Democracy, Human Rights, and Labor have donated funds to the Tor network for the last four years. They support the ability of the network to help the cause of democracy and reporting on human rights violations in repressive regimes around the globe. Other notable sponsors past and present include the National Science Foundation, DARPA, Google, and the Federal Foreign Office of Germany. Edward Snowden, the controversial NSA whistleblower, used Tor in June 2013 to anonymously provide confidential data to reporters from the *Washington Post* and the British newspaper *The Guardian*.

If we look at the other side of the coin, there are reports of the Tor network being used for trafficking in child pornography content and open markets for drugs, stolen credit cards, and other illegal goods and services. In combination with hosting a site on the Tor network, money can change hands anonymously using a peer-to-peer cryptocurrency like Bitcoin. This creates a challenge for law enforcement officials in their efforts to identify criminals and collect tangible evidence. The Tor network is commonly used in the operation of the "Dark Web."

THE SILK ROAD

One Tor site has gained particular notoriety, the now defunct Silk Road. Hailed as the first modern darknet market, it was launched in 2011 and allowed for buying and selling of drugs until its shutdown in October 2013. A user would visit the site by using a special browser and navigating to Silkroad6ownowfk.onion. This marketplace was a pioneer in the "Wild, Wild West" of the dark web, and developed into a successful enterprise through the revolutionary combination of Tor network anonymity, Bitcoin currency anonymity, and peer buyer and seller reviews. A repeat customer of a drug dealer on the website could anonymously visit the site, exchange funds for drugs, yet still leave authenticated reviews, which other potential buyers could see in their searches within the marketplace.

The anonymous team hosting the Silk Road actively managed the marketplace, policing buyers and sellers, and maintained a Terms of Service which restricted the buying and selling of certain goods, such as child pornography, stolen credit cards, or weapons of any kind. However, this didn't stop some of those from using the site.

USING NODES AND HIDDEN SERVERS

When you open a web browser and navigate to a public website or hidden Tor website, your traffic is encrypted from end-to-end through successive layers of encryption, through a series of nodes connecting you to your ultimate destination. Each node only gets enough information so that it can pass the message on to the next node, a process that is repeated in reverse when traffic is passed back from the server to the requesting user.

Hidden services are anonymous websites that exist solely on the dark web, using special hosting software so that all traffic is encrypted coming in or out. Maintaining anonymity for hidden services requires special configuration to ensure the underlying public Internet IP address is not exposed, and thereby unmasking the location of the site. We discussed this process earlier in the chapter on cryptography. There are various free packages offered online for the purpose of making it easier to use the Tor network, such as the Tails operating system (The Amnesiac Incognito Live System) and the Tor browser, a specially adapted version of Firefox.

Leaked information from NSA documents indicate that visitors to Tor-related websites, like https://www.torproject.org, are monitored and may incur additional tracking due to their interest in this technology, under a program known as XKeyScore. Yes, the federal government, regardless of their funding contributions to Tor, see the users of the system as potential criminals or terrorists and want to know who you are and what you are doing. It is important to realize that not only government agencies but also private organizations concerned with security need to be concerned with Tor network entry and exit portals or similar technologies. Information that can enter or exit a network without being verified poses a risk to proprietary information as well as information that an organization may be mandated to protect.

UNMASKING TOR USERS

In the quest to bring criminals to justice, the FBI and law enforcement face unprecedented challenges with collecting evidence from the Tor network. In the case of criminals and pranksters using the public web, an LEO agent can serve a hosting provider like Twitter or Google with a subpoena, and gather the source IP addresses used to commit a crime. Correlating that with subscriber information maintained by the ISP that owns those addresses, pinpointing the originating offender becomes a trivial exercise.

The difficulty that the Tor network introduces is that the originating IP address associated with a crime may be a Tor exit node, having no relationship with the perpetrator, and there are several public incidences of police acting on limited technical understanding as they arrest exit node operators. All of this leaves the identity of a criminal using the Tor network as a mystery, but as history shows us, there is no guarantee of anonymity when the FBI becomes committed to taking down an illegal hidden site.

In September 2013, the FBI issued an arrest warrant for Ross Ulbricht, believed to be the mastermind behind the Silk Road website. The FBI identified the true IP address used to host the Silk Road website, and through it they were able to gather evidence that Mr. Ulbricht (aka "Dread Pirate Roberts"), was involved in hosting the site. There are conflicting reports that account for the FBI's ability to unmask the hidden service. They claim that a misconfigured CAPTCHA page contained the IP address; however, researchers and lawyers for the defendant's claim that someone hacked the php software used to host the site, which ultimately revealed the underlying IP address.

As law enforcement and other government agencies continue to look for new ways to unmask Tor users and hidden sites, they contribute to an ongoing arms race in anonymization technology. As soon as one unmasking technique is used, and inevitably made public, this opens a brief window into the inner-workings of the dark web, after which security professionals rush to patch the hole, and so on.

CONCLUSION

The Internet is much like an iceberg. Only a small part of it is visible at any given point of time to the general user. It is the hidden part that drives hackers, criminals, terrorists, and investigators. You have to know what you are looking for to get inside the really interesting parts of the web, but in doing so you open yourself up to being flagged for subsequent monitoring by law enforcement and other government agencies like the NSA.

Of course there is no way any type of legislative system can keep up with the speed at which the web changes. No sooner is some hidden part exposed than the breech is patched. As soon as a business is hacked, the IT team moves in to seal the opening and shut out the attacker—hopefully before the hacker gets to anything sensitive. Often, no matter how hard organizations try, the hacker, criminal, or terrorist makes it completely inside and pulls out the most sensitive of secrets.

QUESTIONS FOR FURTHER CONSIDERATION

1. Describe the underlying technologies that developed into our modern Internet. How do these technologies continue to contribute to the modern Internet?

2. How could software that shares underlying technology still affect us today?

3. How did the lack of security design in the early Internet still affect our modern web? How could it have been changed?

4. Does a failure to embedding security have modern trends that can be reversed and how?

5. How did the underlying ease of accessibility affect our modern web? How well was it planned?

6. Since the Internet is a compilation of many other inventions and technologies, how can the development of the Internet be compared to other inventions?

7. Can a crime committed, via the Internet, in one nation be prosecuted in another? Will both countries be held to the same standard? How does this come into play as cloud providers move data across international boundaries? Provide references in this answer.

REFERENCES

Andreessen, Marc and Eric Bina. 1994. NCSA Mosaic: A Global Hypermedia System. *Internet Research* 4 (1): 7–17.

Campbell, Matthew, Jeremy Hodges, and Alex Webb. 2015. "TalkTalk Attack Shows Firms Have No Place to Hide From Hackers." Blomberg Technology (October 25). https://www.bloomberg.com/news/articles/2015-10-25/talktalk-attack-shows-firms-have-no-place-to-hide-from-hackers.

Cox, Joseph. 2015. "The People Who Risk Jail to Maintain the Tor Network." Motherboard, The VICE Channels (April 27). http://motherboard.vice.com/read/the-operators.

Dougherty, Carter and Grace Huang. 2014. "Mt. Gox Seeks Bankruptcy After $480 Million Bitcoin Loss." Blomberg Technology (February 28). https://www.bloomberg.com/news/articles/2014-02-28/mt-gox-exchange-files-for-bankruptcy.

FCC 15-24. In the Matter of Protecting and Promoting the Open Internet, GN Docket No. 14-28. https://apps.fcc.gov/edocs_public/attachmatch/FCC-15-24A1.pdf.

Green, Thomas C. 2003. *Chapter One: Kevin Mitnick's story* (January 13). http://www.theregister.co.uk/2003/01/13/chapter_one_kevin_mitnicks_story/.

ICT Facts and Figures 2016. http://www.itu.int/en/ITU-D/Statistics/Documents/facts/ICTFactsFigures2016.pdf.

Kleinman, Zoe. 2013. "Luxury toilet users warned of hardware flaw." BBC News (August 5). http://www.bbc.com/news/technology-23575249.

McGrath, Maggie. 2014. "Target Data Breach Spilled Info On As Many As 70 Million Customers." *Forbes* (January 10). http://www.forbes.com/sites/maggiemcgrath/2014/01/10/target-data-breach-spilled-info-on-as-many-as-70-million-customers/#1fd41b326bd1.

OpenSignal.com State of Mobile Networks. https://opensignal.com/reports/2016/08/usa/state-of-the-mobile-network/.

Phelps, Jordyn. 2016. "Obama tells Putin Hackers Shouldn't Create Cyber 'Wild Wild West.'" ABC News (September 5). http://abcnews.go.com/Politics/president-obama-syria-havent-closed-gaps-reaching-deal/story?id=41866362.

Poushter, Jacob. 2016. "Smartphone Ownership and Internet Usage Continues to Climb in Emerging Economies." Pew Research Center (February 22). http://www.pewglobal.org/2016/02/22/smartphone-ownership-and-internet-usage-continues-to-climb-in-emerging-economies/.

STRATFOR. 2016. SITREP. U.S.: Internet of Things Partly Responsible for Cyberattack (October 22). https://www.stratfor.com/situation-report/us-internet-things-partly-responsible-cyberattack.

Symbolics.com. http://www.uwhois.com/cgi/whois.cgi?query=symbolics.com.

Tarbell, Christopher. 2013. Sealed Complaint (September 27). http://krebsonsecurity.com/wp-content/uploads/2013/10/UlbrichtCriminalComplaint.pdf.

Tor. Tor Sponsors. https://www.torproject.org/about/sponsors.html.en.

Waldrop, Mitch. Darpa and the Internet Revolution. *50 Years of Bridging the Gap*. http://www.darpa.mil/attachments/(2O15)%20Global%20Nav%20-%20About%20Us%20-%20History%20-%20Resources%20-%2050th%20-%20Internet%20(Approved).pdf.

CHAPTER 10

THE HUMAN SIDE OF CYBERSECURITY

KEY WORDS

Access	Authentication	Data Breech
Access Control	Blacklist	Whitelist
Access Control Lists	CIO	

THE CLASSICS ARE STILL GOOD REFERENCES

In 1983 a high school student, David Lightman, was considering ways to examine and play new and unique computer games that had yet to be released by their developers. He uses a home setup of computers and phone modems to "dial in" to the external connection of these companies then guessed at passwords for backdoor access. Lightman ultimately works his way into a software design company that wrote the programming to operate the WOPR (War Operation Plan Response) computer system, supposedly used to directly control launch of the US land-based nuclear arsenal. Through a backdoor and guessed password he gains access to "Joshua," what he believes is a new computer game program that includes "Global Thermonuclear War" as an option. He starts the game process without realizing that he is activating the WOPR to proceed with an automatic detection and response procedure that will ultimately result in a full-scale nuclear attack on the Soviet Union.

Sounds like a nightmare of a problem, doesn't it? It makes for a great movie plot, one that has been reproduced any number of times across multiple different versions based on evolving technology. While the Lightman–WOPR incident takes place in 1983, the basis of the technology necessary to remotely access computers, software, and data is relatively similar today. The ultimate vulnerability in the movie *War Games* is still the primary concern for security managers and CIOs today. The problem isn't the software, it's the people.

DATA THIEVES

Edward Snowden is a former National Security Agency (NSA) subcontractor who stole and then leaked over 1.5 million classified documents from secure NSA networks, including information on the PRISM program that allowed real-time information collection on American citizens electronically. The House Intelligence Committee released a report September 15, 2016, that characterized Snowden as a "disgruntled employee who had frequent conflicts with his managers," a "serial exaggerator and fabricator," and "not a whistle-blower." The US spent hundreds of millions of dollars investigating the Snowden breech and analyzing the impact of the loss of data. Snowden gained access to these files by using logon credentials of his colleagues and his access as a systems administrator to concurrently remove personal identifiable information of thousands of IC employees and contractors.

Figure 10.1   By NSA, US Federal Government; original (C) Adam Hart-Davis © 1998-04-08—http://www.washingtonpost.com/wp-srv/special/politics/prism-collection-documents/, Public Domain, https://commons.wikimedia.org/w/index.php?curid=26554779

Bradley (aka Chelsea Elizabeth) Manning, a US Army intelligence analyst, had legitimate access to hundreds of thousands of data files and videos as a function of his job in Iraq. In 2010 he passed to the organization Wikileaks a massive amount of classified material that included military field operations reports, US State Department cables, and raw intelligence data including a video of US helicopter gunships attacking unarmed peaceful gatherings in Iraq. After having attacked his commanding officer, Manning, who was facing a dishonorable discharge, was caught not by the actions of professional investigators or by the Army's cybersecurity professionals, but by a civilian hacker in whom he confided. That hacker, Adrian Lamo, informed the US Army of what Manning had confided concerning his theft and sharing of the data.

In the first eleven (11) months of 2016 there were 4,903,563 individual records with personal identification information that were breeched in over 470 events. Among these were the Google Android system with over a million records breeched, the US Navy Career Waypoints Database with over 134,000 personal records of sailors stolen from a contractor's laptop, and an

Figure 10.2   Bradley Manning.

unknown number of Internal Revenue Service (IRS) taxpayer records that could potentially affect up to 28.2 million people. Other data breeches in 2016 include Michigan State University; Eye Institute of Marin, California; Springfield Armory; Luque Chiropactic, Inc., California; QVC, Inc.; FriendFinder, California (over 412 million records affected); UFCW Local 655, Food Employers Joint Pension Plan; Pace University, NY; Office of the Comptroller of the Currency, Washington, D.C.; and Weebly, California (over 43 million website builder records affected). That's just the past thirty days before writing this chapter!!!

DATA BREECH
loss of access control over data due to unauthorized internal or external access. Usually associated with the loss of significant personnel, technical, or business information that may prove detrimental to the agency, corporation, or government.

From 2005 to the end of November 2016 there were 564 insider attacks affecting over 36,274,000 records. Another 952 unintended disclosures affecting nearly 33,000,000 records. The loss of almost 176,000,000 records due to the loss of nearly 1,750 portable devices and paper files. And these are just the publically reported losses!!

At this point you are probably wondering how much of your personal information is out there on the web, let alone how much of your company data. Personally, the authors' information has been lost by or stolen from the US government so many times that we are no longer tracking the events. Instead, both authors have moved into safeguarding our personal account data by constantly modifying and updating passwords and other identifier information used to gain access to critical information and accounts. We utilize third-party monitoring and protection software and companies to constantly review the Internet for indications of threats to our data, and immediately take action to change logon information, change accounts, report thefts, etc., whenever something pops up indicating we have been compromised.

We strongly recommend that you do the same personally and for your agency. It is worth the expense and the effort. Unless you can cover the cost of recovering your identity, correcting financial records, correcting Social Security records, your banking information, and have a bank that limits your liability for loss, paying for protection AND recovery is an imperative in today's world.

PROTECTING YOUR AGENCY'S INFORMATION

Every agency and organization is different. Thus, while some groups have extensive IT departments with large numbers of people to control and monitor employee access, others will have a single person, or maybe two, working under a manager that is responsible for a wide variety of other duties. For example, one of the authors works for a university that has IT as a component within the Vice President of Accounting and Financial Affairs unit. IT and Software are separate divisions, one of which works under Institutional Effectiveness. Thus, the people that control and operate the systems that provide computer and account access to faculty, staff, and students is separate from those that are designing software necessary to course delivery and recordkeeping. There is no Chief Information Officer **(CIO)** at the University. So, here arises the question: who is responsible for information security? The answer: We don't know.

CHIEF INFORMATION OFFICER (CIO)
Agency official responsible for: (1) providing advice or other assistance to the head of the executive agency and other senior management personnel of the agency to ensure that information systems are acquired and information resources are managed in a manner that is consistent with laws, Executive Orders, directives, policies, regulations, and priorities established by the head of the agency; (2) developing, maintaining, and facilitating the implementation of a sound and integrated information system architecture for the agency; and (3) promoting the effective and efficient design and operation of all major information resources management processes for the agency, including improvements to work processes of the agency.

AUTHENTICATION
Verifying the identity of a user, process, or device, often as a prerequisite to allowing access to resources in an information system.

ACCESS CONTROL
The process of granting or denying specific requests to: (1) obtain and use information and related information processing services; and (2) enter specific facilities.

ACCESS CONTROL LISTS (ACLS)
A register of: (1) users (including groups, machines, processes) who have been given permission to use a particular system resource; and (2) the types of access they have been permitted.

Somebody at your organization is responsible for organizational information security. That person controls who gets **access** to your systems and data. They establish the system of **authentication** and **access control** and maintain and update the **access control lists** (ACLs) for the agency. Whether you have a high level of personnel turnover—or only gain and lose people occasionally, it becomes essential that your ACLs are not only updated regularly, but the level of access to information is monitored and limited to those with a need to know. We know, we know—your agency may not have highly classified information, or records that require limited access. That doesn't mean you shouldn't be secure!

Remember Chapter 1—we are only as secure as we make ourselves. Having locks on the outside doors doesn't mean you don't need to close and lock the jewelry safe in the master bedroom closet. Just because you trust the housekeeper from some third world country to access your home and clean the rooms doesn't mean you trust them to rummage through your personal financial papers whenever they want. You may give a house guest a spare key so they can come and go as they please, but you don't hand them the combination to your firearms safe! The situation is no different at your place of work.

The data entry clerk at the Department of Motor Vehicles has a tremendous amount of information at their fingertips. Yet their password is nothing more than their child's name and birth date. The businessman opening that new account at the bank has a unique eastern European name and looks over the shoulder of the account manager as she enters the system to enter his data. Your police department is so embarrassed by a wrongful arrest of an 88-year-old woman that the hard drive containing the arrest and processing videos just happens to suffer a catastrophic failure, losing all the data it contained, including an unknown number of records for ongoing criminal prosecutions. These are all real incidents that resulted in the loss of data and the theft of millions (perhaps billions) of dollars from ATM machines over two years, with $13 million on one day in Japan. Almost makes you want to become a criminal hacker—but only for a day . . .

Here is the problem—people are people and will always make mistakes. No matter how much you train or educate your staff (or yourself), those that want to do you harm will always be out there. The question is how much of a trade-off is necessary to ensure sufficient compartmentalization to protect the data from the unauthorized while maintaining sufficient data availability to ensure continued smooth organizational operations. We, the authors, don't have an answer. Perhaps your insurance company has one. Ultimately, what level of risk they are willing to accept is the determiner of what cost you will incur in the process of conducting operations. Lawsuits for losing data can be very expensive.

IMPROVING DATA PROTECTION

Let's reconsider the DMV data entry clerk mentioned above. Is the problem her password or your system of authentication? She needs access to the software to be able to do her job. You need to secure the data in the system to prevent unauthorized access. She doesn't want a difficult password to have to remember and you don't want her using a password that is easily compromised. The solution may be as simple as adding an extra level of authentication to the access process. Perhaps something as simple as an individual biometric fingerprint scanner along with her password. That way, even with somebody looking over her shoulder or observing her keystrokes while entering a password wouldn't provide a single point of breech.

What about that police department hard drive? A hard drive rarely suffers a complete failure. Even when the drive fails, the data is still there and can be recovered forensically. In the past we would take magnetic drives or magnetic tape drives and wipe the data by placing them on a powerful magnetic device. This essentially erased or scrambled the data such that it was functionally gone. With modern, solid-state hard drives, the data is still there, even if the reader/writer is broken. Instead of disposing of the drive, establish strict accounting protocols that limit physical access to the hard drives. Require log entries for all persons with access to these devices and the places where they are stored. Any work on the drive, including removal and replacement, would necessitate the use of two-person control and packaging and shipping of the device to a data recovery company. That company could then recover the data remaining on the drive, write it to a new drive, and return it to your agency along with the original damaged drive. Additionally, create strict policies that require the immediate termination of any person that violates the protocol. Your insurance company that provides coverage for the agency/city can offer you some excellent advice in this area and it might just save you a lot of money in comparison with the cost of the added controls.

I don't know about you, but anytime banks lose millions of dollars due to ATM fraud I get worried about my own bank account. Once again—this becomes an issue of people and control of passwords and access. For only a small portion of the lost money the South African bank could have implemented multiple authentication controls to prevent the creation of fake accounts and issuance of associated credit and ATM cards. Instead, the bank chose to go with the easy route and only require passwords for those people who create new accounts for customers—usually some of the lowest paid bank employees and those with the highest turnover. It makes you wonder about the focus of the bank management when they eliminate essential account controls in favor of profit margins. Who are they trying to please? The stockholders or the bank customers? I believe that I'd be looking for a new place to put my money . . .

SOCIAL ENGINEERING PROBLEMS

Over 91 percent of outside attacks begin with a phishing or spear-phishing e-mail. These e-mails usually contain a threat or sense of urgency, have a generic or overly formal salutation or even use your e-mail name as the salutation, and frequently contain grammatical mistakes and spelling errors.

© Rawpixel.com/Shutterstock.com

These are red flags and you should teach your personnel how to identify them. You should also teach them not to click on any links in the e-mail or open or download any files attached to the e-mail. Your people should forward these e-mails intact, with the full header information, to your IT folks for analysis. It doesn't take much to create a system of security awareness within any company or agency and providing incentives to employees for reporting such attacks can be more beneficial than using intimidation or threats.[1] Additional information about social engineering attacks can be found at www.social-engineer.org.

If you are successful in getting your people to address these phishing e-mails, then you will probably be successful in preventing them from downloading ransomware. This is the second largest source of data loss and financial loss to corporations/agencies. Addressing this issue requires you to go beyond the ordinary level of protection and ensure that employees do not use company/agency computers to access social media or Internet information. Just as important is that you prevent employees from connecting any unscanned portable storage devices to the system. At the Federal Emergency Management Agency's National Emergency Training Center they have instituted a strict policy where no USB device will work in any computer on-site unless it has been previously scanned and authorized by the IT department. Some organizations have gone so far as to only allow USB drives that they provide. Additionally, they have put blocks on

1. Basic e-mail tips can be found at https://securingthehuman.sans.org/newsletters/ouch/issues/ OUCH-201407_en.pdf#__utma=216335632.2054005874.1480821707.1480821707.1480821707.1 &__utmb=216335632.7.8.1480821800712&__utmc=216335632&__utmx=-&__utmz=216335632. 1480821707.1.1.utmcsr=(direct)|utmccn=(direct)|utmcmd=(none)&__utmv=-&_utmk=242812097.

the system so that you cannot access e-mail hosting sites like Google Mail (g-mail), Yahoo, or Hotmail. With literally tens of thousands of students coming from all around the world annually, this process is an essential step to protect their data management systems. It causes problems and difficulty for students, but saves the federal government from recovery costs should they suffer a system breach.

One of the easy ways we can create these types of protection at our homes and places of work is to utilize the Whitelist and Blacklist functions on our ISPs and e-mail programs. Every program has a different means of implementing these so rather than try to describe them, let's just describe the functions. A **whitelist** is sort of an "approved sender" list that indicates to your screening software that e-mail from these sources is acceptable. Typically when an address hits the whitelist it never goes to the blacklist as it has been "pre-approved" for your usage.

A **blacklist** is just the opposite, a list of "blocked" e-mail senders. Some programs will allow you to directly add a sender to the blacklist by simply clicking your junk button. Others require you to formally add the sender to the blocked list. It all depends on the type of software you are using.

It is important to mention that whitelists are accessed first and blacklists are then checked, so an address listed in both black and whitelists will be allowed almost every time.

There is also a means to block certain websites. Usually this is performed in the parental guidance function on a computer. If you are in a small agency without a regular IT department you can use this existing system to limit Internet access to all employee computers. If you are in an organization or agency with a formally established and capable IT department you can ask your IT people to prevent access to social networking sites, YouTube, outside e-mail systems, etc., through their management software. They will understand what you want and can make it happen. They can also install tracking software to rapidly identify users that try to circumvent the blocks or who are using proxy servers to side-step established protocols.

As with all things related to cybersecurity the majority of the problems reside in the people. If the software engineers would write software from scratch, rather than using predeveloped software packages to splice code components, then many of the problems inherent today would go away. If people would use their gray matter to evaluate the potential outcomes of their actions, then ransomware and phishing would also go away. Unfortunately, the cybersecurity manager cannot depend on either of these actions ever working. There is, however, a simple and effective way to teach your people how to establish memorable yet mostly secure passwords. There are

WHITELIST

A list of discrete entities, such as hosts or applications that are known to be benign and are approved for use within an organization and/or information system.

BLACKLIST

A list of discrete entities, such as hosts or applications, that have been previously determined to be associated with malicious activity.

even unique methods that security professionals have created with posters and education pieces ready to be implemented by your organization. Feel free to reference https://www.sans.org/search/results to assist in finding resources to create policies or educational training to improve your overall security posture. Normally SANS simply asks for credit when you reference their work.

SIMPLE AND SECURE PASSWORDS

Most software programs require users to change passwords on a regular basis. Some use a 90-day cycle while others use a 120-day cycle. Others have established formal password change protocols for just prior to a major event, such as when universities require all faculty to change their passwords a week or two before final grades are entered at the end of a semester.

© Evan Lorne/Shutterstock.com

Then there are the programs that never require people to change their passwords, such as Google Mail, banks, investment accounts, Hotmail, AOL, etc. In these cases you can take the time to teach your employees easy means of creating memorable yet difficult to penetrate passwords. Let's say the clerk at the DMV is using her son's name and birthday as a password: jackson1262006, for Jackson as the name, 12 as the month, 6 as the day, and 2006 as the year. It has lowercase letters, numbers, and is fourteen characters in length. Normally this would meet just about every system's protocols. It's not that tough a password to crack for somebody who wants to get into her system. What if you can teach her a better way to create a password that can be changed routinely yet remain memorable? Consider this as an option. On the QWERTY keyboard the appropriate keys to enter her password would be:

!	@	#	$	%	^	&	*	(	)
1	2	3	4	5	6	7	8	9	0
Q	W	E	R	T	Y	U	I	O	P
q	w	e	r	t	y	u	i	o	p
A	S	D	F	G	H	J	K	L	:
a	s	d	f	g	h	j	k	l	;
Z	X	C	V	B	N	M	<	>	?
z	x	c	V	b	n	m	,	.	/

This means the password is constructed of 7 letters (1 uppercase) and 4 numbers. If she was to use the SHIFT key on every other character the new password would be: JaCkSoN1@6@)0^, seven letters (4 uppercase), three numbers, and three special characters. Because of the every other character shift sequence this too is an obvious combination to a person intent on getting access to her system.

How about having her make a couple of additional adjustments to the sequence of keys she enters and have her replace obvious letters with characters that simulate those characters, such as replacing the "A" in Jackson with "@" and the number "1" with a capitol "I" or "!". Now her password would be J@ckson!262006. If she were to change the letter "O" to a zero and the zeros to lowercase "o" and the "s" to "$" then the password becomes even more difficult to break but still as easy to remember: J@ck$0n!262oo6. Now the QWERTY keyboard looks like this:

!	@	#	$	%	^	&	*	(	)
1	2	3	4	5	6	7	8	9	0
Q	W	E	R	T	Y	U	I	O	P
q	w	e	r	t	y	u	i	o	p
A	S	D	F	G	H	J	K	L	:
a	s	d	f	g	h	j	k	l	;
Z	X	C	V	B	N	M	<	>	?
z	x	c	V	b	n	m	,	.	/

The randomization of characters and numbers adds to the complexity of the password while maintaining the simplicity of memorization for the user. To change the password on a regular basis any variation of the letters and symbols would be sufficient without being overly complex to remember yet maintaining a randomization of the mixture of characters, numbers, and upper- and lowercase numbers.

These simple techniques will make it complicated enough that even with a person looking over her shoulder, the DMV clerk's password wouldn't be easily memorized or duplicated.

Of course, the issue of remembering passwords for websites can be very difficult. Particularly when each website uses a different set of approved characters, varying requirements for upper- and lowercase letters, and amount of numbers and in what order they can be used. Alternatively, you could adjust the security system to use a CAPTCHA recognition using varying images that require a person to prove they are not a robot. Or the reading of non-linear letter and number combinations. Or require a separate pin number and security question that varies along with a direct report to IT and the user every time a wrong answer is submitted. You could even establish automatic lock-out for an account after three false entries (happens to us all the time) or use an auto image capture and report for each false entry (happens to us all the time) with a lock-out after three attempts. This may seem like a lot of trouble to protect some basic data—but they are all methods the authors use on their various devices to access the device or some sensitive account (like our bank accounts).

Ultimately, the process of determining the system you will use to ensure your system is secure and protected from intrusion requires decisions on your part. The IT folks will have lots of great ideas, but you still have to remember that the average user isn't going to be an IT person, and will probably be much like the lady in Chapter 2—not even capable of turning on her own computer.

A lot of recent attention has been placed on shifting from passwords to passphrases, which incorporate many of the transliterations listed previously under passwords but instead of the base word of "J@ck$0n!262oo6" it might include a phrase such as "ActionJackson2006" which could be easily altered to "Ac+i0nJ@ck$0n!262oo6" or another nickname which might be easily remembered by the individual, but combines multiple dictionary terms together. This is of course taking for granted that your password system will accept a term of that length. Changing to the concept of a passphrase versus a password exponentially changes the difficulty of cracking the code.

CONCLUSION

Joshua, the WOPR computer in the 1983 movie *War Games* was scary. Today, every computer is scary. The recent IoT attack on the Dyn system shut down Internet access and social media across the East Coast of the US and parts of Europe. If a hacker can execute a DDOS attack against Dyn by infecting toasters with malware that turned them into a botnet, imagine what a country with a cyber-army could do. With all of our information essentially already compromised due to the numbers of data breeches over the past twenty years, it is only a matter of time before your identity is stolen and used against you. Imagine what life would be like if tomorrow none of your credit or debit cards worked, the bank no longer recognized you, your driver's license was canceled along with your auto insurance, and your investments for retirement suddenly disappeared. Do you think that would cause you some stress? What about that happening to all the employees in your company or agency? Would anybody come to work that day or the next or would they all be at their banks trying to prove who they are only to find out the Social Security Administration had them recorded as deceased? Ever try to bring somebody back from the dead? It isn't as easy as it used to be.

This is the reason we must consider that all people are potential problems to our security. We have to have compartmentalized access and restrict the really sensitive information to that rare few who can really be trusted. Not everybody needs access to everything in your agency and not everybody in management needs access to personnel or financial records. When somebody who doesn't need that access gets it do you have systems in place to identify those breeches and lock down systems? We certainly hope you do.

QUESTIONS FOR FURTHER CONSIDERATION

1. When considering a password, what are some rules to consider? Can you create a password using passphrase techniques?

2. Who might be interested in gaining access to your data? Why?

3. If data is considered the new digital currency, is your account empty or full? Explain.

4. Why should you be concerned about the unauthorized collection of your data?

5. What can you do to protect yourself from data loss?

REFERENCES

Kissel, Richard Ed. 2013. *Glossary of Key Information Security Terms.* NISTIR 7298 Rev. 2. Washington, D.C.: U.S. Department of Commerce (May).

Kottasova, Ivana. 2016. "Two hours and 1,600 fake credit cards later: $13 million is gone." *CNN Money* (May 23). CNN.com. http://money.cnn.com/2016/05/23/news/bank-fraud-south-africa-japan/.

Manning, Chelsea. (n.d.). *Bio.com*. A&E Television Networks. http://www.biography.com/people/chelsea-manning-21299995#mannings-future-and-the-leak-aftermath.

Quemere, Andrew and Maya Shaffer. 2016. "Broken Records: The Pitts." *Digboston.com* (April 6). https://digboston.com/broken-records-the-pitts/.

U.S. House of Representatives. 2016. *Executive Summary of Review of the Unauthorized Disclosures of Former National Security Agency Contractor Edward Snowden*. Washington, D.C.: House of Representatives (September 15).

War Games. 1983. MGM, United Artists. http://www.imdb.com/title/tt0086567/.

CHAPTER 11

THE GOVERNMENT

KEY WORDS

CFAA	Computer Forensics	Jurisdiction
Child Pornography	Fraud	Privacy

JURISDICTION
Where a crime takes place.

FRAUD
The act of using a computer to take or alter electronic data, or to gain unlawful use of a computer or system.

CFAA
Fraud and related activity in connection with computers.

As we've already discussed, technology provides criminals with new opportunities, and many existing laws do not adequately address the use of computers. Prosecution of crimes such as child exploitation, theft of intellectual property, Internet fraud, and cyberstalking has yet to be resolved, for any number of reasons. One issue is **jurisdiction**. If an Internet fraud is conducted in one state, via an offshore ISP, against a victim in another state—who has jurisdiction? Where did the crime take place? A related issue is extradition of criminals from other countries. Legislation covering computer misuse has matured but continues to evolve as case law and technology develop. In the US, computer fraud and abuse are defined and addressed by 18 U.S. Code § 1030—**Fraud** and related activity in connection with computers (also known as **CFAA**) at the federal level, and by state law for the remainder of smaller offenses. In the UK and EU, fraud, forgery, and computer misuse are defined slightly differently.

© Parkheta/Shutterstock.com

18 U.S. CODE § 1030—FRAUD AND RELATED ACTIVITY IN CONNECTION WITH COMPUTERS

(a) Whoever—

(1) having knowingly accessed a computer without authorization or exceeding authorized access, and by means of such conduct having obtained information that has been determined by the United States Government pursuant to an Executive order or statute to require protection against unauthorized disclosure for reasons of national defense or foreign relations, or any restricted data, as defined in paragraph y. of section 11 of the Atomic Energy Act of 1954, with reason to believe that such information so obtained could be used to the injury of the United States, or to the advantage of any foreign nation willfully communicates, delivers, transmits, or causes to be communicated, delivered, or transmitted, or attempts to communicate, deliver, transmit or cause to be communicated, delivered, or transmitted the same to any person not entitled to receive it, or willfully retains the same and fails to deliver it to the officer or employee of the United States entitled to receive it;

(2) intentionally accesses a computer without authorization or exceeds authorized access, and thereby obtains—

(A) information contained in a financial record of a financial institution, or of a card issuer as defined in section 1602(n) [1] of title 15, or contained in a file of a consumer reporting agency on a consumer, as such terms are defined in the Fair Credit Reporting Act (15 U.S.C. 1681 et seq.);

(B) information from any department or agency of the United States; or

(C) information from any protected computer;

(3) intentionally, without authorization to access any nonpublic computer of a department or agency of the United States, accesses such a computer of that department or agency that is exclusively for the use of the Government of the United States or, in the case of a computer not exclusively for such use, is used by or for the Government of the United States and such conduct affects that use by or for the Government of the United States;

(4) knowingly and with intent to defraud, accesses a protected computer without authorization, or exceeds authorized access, and by means of such conduct furthers the intended fraud and obtains anything of value, unless the object of the fraud and the thing obtained consists only of the use of the computer and the value of such use is not more than $5,000 in any 1-year period;

(5)

(A) knowingly causes the transmission of a program, information, code, or command, and as a result of such conduct, intentionally causes damage without authorization, to a protected computer;

(B) intentionally accesses a protected computer without authorization, and as a result of such conduct, recklessly causes damage; or

(C) intentionally accesses a protected computer without authorization, and as a result of such conduct, causes damage and loss.[2]

(6) knowingly and with intent to defraud traffics (as defined in section 1029) in any password or similar information through which a computer may be accessed without authorization, if—

(A) such trafficking affects interstate or foreign commerce; or

(B) such computer is used by or for the Government of the United States; [3]

(7) with intent to extort from any person any money or other thing of value, transmits in interstate or foreign commerce any communication containing any—

(A) threat to cause damage to a protected computer;

(B) threat to obtain information from a protected computer without authorization or in excess of authorization or to impair the confidentiality of information obtained from a protected computer without authorization or by exceeding authorized access; or

(C) demand or request for money or other thing of value in relation to damage to a protected computer, where such damage was caused to facilitate the extortion; shall be punished as provided in subsection (c) of this section.

Current through Public Law 114-38.

The United States Secret Service has primary authority for investigating computer crime in the United States except for cases of espionage, foreign counterintelligence, information protected against unauthorized disclosure for reasons of national defense or foreign relations, or Restricted Data (as defined under the Atomic Energy Act of 1954), which are investigated by the FBI. Punishments for violations of the CFAA vary on the specific section and subsection, but essentially run from one to twenty years and accompanying fines.

CHILD PORNOGRAPHY

CHILD PORNOGRAPHY
Realistic images representing a minor engaged in sexually explicit conduct.

Another issue is the varying definitions of, and the confusion between, "pornography," **"child pornography,"** and "obscenity." The Child Pornography Protection Act was overturned by the Supreme Court. The Congress then passed the Child Online Protection Act, which was also held in abeyance, was replaced by the Children's Internet Protection Act which is not yet determined to be either constitutional or unconstitutional but is being evaluated by lower courts as it applies to data filters on public computers at libraries and schools that might be used by children. The US has always had a problem determining what was and wasn't pornographic or harmful to children and the continuing advances in Internet technology has not made this process any easier.

In regard to child pornography, at present in the US "virtual" child pornography is still protected by the First Amendment. CPPA was an unsuccessful attempt to remove this protection, the premise being that child pornography, real or digitally created, was inherently evil. However, under UK law "pseudo-photographs" are considered illegal, and the European Council's Cybercrime Convention Committee includes "realistic images representing a minor engaged in sexually explicit conduct" in their definition of child pornography. The rationale for making virtual child pornography illegal is that it increases the availability of such materials and thereby increases the demand. A counterargument is that law enforcement may not be able to distinguish between virtual versus real child pornography, making it more difficult to address the illegal activities. Sentencing guidelines for child pornography convictions continues to be an area of controversy, and the discussion about sentencing in the UK is provided to stimulate discussion.

PRIVACY INTRUSIONS

Our "right to privacy" is an equally ambiguous concept. From a legal standpoint it is:

1. The right to be free from governmental intrusion (protected by the Constitution) and

2. The protection from intrusion into our private lives by others (protected by common law).

Although search and seizure requirements and procedures in the US and UK are very similar, in Europe, personal data are protected by an EU directive and by associated legislation in individual countries. Historically, the EU has offered greater **privacy** protection than the US, making it more difficult for entities in these two to exchange associated data. However, in response to increases in international terrorism, some EU countries are considering legislation to give authorities greater access to personal data. This continuing conflict between what is acceptable evidence under one judicial system being unacceptable under another judicial system simply complicates the situation.

This raises the question—to what do we have a reasonable expectation of privacy? If you are in your home, taking a shower, you can expect that somebody filming you would be violating your privacy. However, if you are using a pay-to-view website where you can watch the daily activities of an Internet celebrity, and you watch them while they shower, dress, cook, sleep, or have sex, have you violated their expectation to privacy? How would you know what the law is based on the country of origin and all the various countries the imagery transited to get to your computer? Do you have an expectation that since you are a paying customer of the site you have a right to privacy when it comes to a potential investigation into your behavior? What if that behavior is indicative of criminality?

PRIVACY
From a legal standpoint it is: the right to be free from governmental intrusion (protected by the Constitution) and the protection from intrusion into our private lives by others (protected by common law).

© Peshkova/Shutterstock.com

What if you are in a foreign country, for example the United Arab Emirates, where everything you read on the Internet comes through government systems that monitor and restrict your access? If you try to view a sex education film in some countries, you find that all the websites are blocked by the government under morality statutes. If you repetitively try to circumvent these blocks, the government sends police to your home or hotel to ask you why you are doing this. They can arbitrarily confiscate your computer and all your electronic devices and view anything they want without warrant or reason. Now, consider that you are just passing through the country on your way to India . . . Do you still expect that the local morality laws won't be enforced?

What if you send an e-mail? Some countries read all the e-mail send into or out of or through their country looking for violations of morality and criminal law. Do you have the same expectation of privacy in the UAE as you had in the US? Should you? At what point does the intrusion into your communications become a problem? As one student said, "I have nothing to worry about because I'm not doing anything wrong." My reply was, "According to who?"

In a globalized world, where the Internet can be used around the world to instantly access information, share data, commit crimes, or conduct warfare, the inability of traditional legal systems to keep up with a system that is changing at the speed of light simply makes any attempt to establish common rules of legality and privacy a near impossibility.

INTELLECTUAL PROPERTY THEFT

Intellectual property theft is based on copyright law. Alex Haley was accused of plagiarizing parts of his epic *Roots*. Napster, KaZaA, and other peer-to-peer applications engaged in the unauthorized distribution (sharing) of copyrighted music. Legal definitions are, again, behind the times. If a data thief breaks into a computer and copies confidential data, is it theft? Theft implies that the owner of the property has been denied its use. The data is intact and still in place. When "data" is stolen, but not removed or altered in any way on the original computer, has the owner of the data been deprived of its use?

Then arises the issue of what is covered by copyright law. If you haven't filed for actual copyright status for the information you have created, is it really protected? Again, that depends on the country involved. Copyright infringement is almost always an issue for Civil Courts—not criminal courts. Thus, recovery of damages caused by result of data theft falls to the person that lost the data to take legal action and sue in the appropriate court and jurisdiction. If your business is in San Angelo, Texas, in the US, and some Nigerian princess hacks your corporate computer and steals the plans for a new process to turn lead into gold—how are you going to even begin the process of getting that supposed princess identified let alone brought to the US, then Texas, and then San Angelo to confront her in the appropriate court?

As you can see, the legal questions about Internet crime are essentially endless. You cannot depend on the federal government to address this type of criminal behavior unless it affects their own computer systems. You can report the behavior. You can bring legal action against the perpetrators, but don't expect much out of the government.

COMPUTER FORENSICS FOR MANAGERS

So—somebody has hacked your system or you have a worm or perhaps ransomware in your hard drive. Now what do you do? As the manager that runs the overall IT unit, there are a few basic steps essential to any investigation that you should consider. However, remember that anything you do to process a search and clean of the system may well destroy evidence that would be required to pursue a legal resolution to your loss.

First, we have to establish some basics. When a crime happens, the crime scene is examined for trace evidence that helps to explain the crime, actions of actors, motives, etc. The same process applies with computer crime. We call this process forensics. **Computer forensics** is the process of using scientific knowledge for collecting, analyzing, and presenting evidence to the courts. (The word *forensics* means "to bring to the court.") Forensics deals primarily with the recovery and analysis of latent evidence. Latent evidence can take many forms, from fingerprints left on a window to DNA evidence recovered from blood stains to the files on a hard drive.

COMPUTER FORENSICS
The main purpose is to identify, collect, preserve, and analyze data in a way that preserves the integrity of the evidence collected so it can be used effectively in a legal case.

Any number of automated forensic tools are available for providing data and computer security; however, it is absolutely crucial that your IT people understand what these tools are doing. The best way to gain that understanding is by experimentation. Before your people jump into hunting for an intruder or some files that might be left behind, they should know how to create a file and viewing the results, delete the file and viewing those results, use a low-level hex editor, and carve data associated with the file into a new one.

Adding the ability to practice sound computer forensics will help you ensure the overall integrity and survivability of your network infrastructure. You can help your organization if you consider computer forensics as a new basic element in what is known as a "defense-in-depth" approach to network and computer security. For instance, understanding the legal and technical aspects of computer forensics will help you capture vital information if your network is compromised and will help you prosecute the case if the intruder is caught.

One way an intruder can cause havoc is with a "keylogger," a program installed on your computer that logs your keystrokes. You can imagine the problems this could cause. Another trick is hiding a file within a picture—steganography. The process is extraordinarily simple nowadays. It is a trick used by pornographers, among others. This means that just because a file appears to be one thing, like a photograph (jpg, bmp, etc.) doesn't mean that is all it might be.

What happens if you ignore computer forensics or practice it badly? You risk destroying vital evidence or having forensic evidence ruled inadmissible in a court of law. Also, you or your organization may run afoul of new laws that mandate regulatory compliance and assign liability if certain types of data are not adequately protected. Recent legislation makes it possible to hold organizations liable in civil or criminal court if they fail to protect customer data.[1]

From a technical standpoint, the main goal of computer forensics is to identify, collect, preserve, and analyze data in a way that preserves the integrity of the evidence collected so it can be used effectively in a legal case. That is what a government investigator is trying to accomplish by gathering forensic evidence; to make a case for court. You, however, may want a different approach.

As the IT manager, the intrusion into your system might just warrant you looking for the hole and patching it. Recovering essential data that has been destroyed or misplaced. Finding and eliminating malware. This is where you make the first decision: what is the primary intent of my investigation? The first step—preserve the evidence so that you can use it later. This will require the IT people to make a complete mirror image of the locations to be inspected—before they start their search for the problem. This allows them to save the persistent data that is stored on the hard drive (or other medium) and is preserved when a computer is turned off. Second, they have to save the volatile data that is stored in memory, or exists in transit, that will be lost when the computer loses power or is turned off. The volatile data resides in registries, cache, and random access memory (RAM). Volatile data is ephemeral and requires somebody that knows how to prevent its loss to act to save it for future examination and use. This is so important that when computer crimes are investigated by the government one of the first acts is to ensure that volatile data is saved and computers and power are sustained in an operational condition (still running if they are on when a warrant is executed) with all sorts of back-up power devices in place for portable memory devices and external drives.

---

1. Laws such as the Health Insurance Portability and Accountability Act (HIPAA), Sarbanes-Oxley, California Act 1798, and others hold businesses liable for breaches in the security or integrity of computer networks.

Third, the system administrators and security personnel must also have a basic understanding of how routine computer and network administrative tasks can affect both the forensic process (the potential admissibility of evidence at court) and the subsequent ability to recover data that may be critical to the identification and analysis of a security incident. These auto-save and auto-update systems have to be turned off for the computers affected by the breech at least until the technicians can save the volatile and persistent data in an unchanged form.

LEGAL ASPECTS OF COMPUTER FORENSICS

Anyone overseeing network security must be aware of the legal implications of forensic activity. Security professionals need to consider their policy decisions and technical actions in the context of existing laws. For instance, you must have authorization before you monitor and collect information related to a computer intrusion. There are also legal ramifications to using security monitoring tools.

Computer forensics is a relatively new discipline to the courts and many of the existing laws used to prosecute computer-related crimes, legal precedents, and practices related to computer forensics are in a state of flux. New court rulings are issued that affect how computer forensics is applied. The best source of information in this area is the United States Department of Justice's Cyber Crime web site (www.justice.gov). The site lists recent court cases involving computer forensics and computer crime, and it has guides about how to introduce computer evidence in court and what standards apply. The important point for forensics investigators is that evidence must be collected in a way that is legally admissible in a court case.

Increasingly, laws are being passed that require organizations to safeguard the privacy of personal data. It is becoming necessary to prove that your organization is complying with computer security best practices. If there is an incident that affects critical data, for instance, the organization that has added a computer forensics capability to its arsenal will be able to show that it followed a sound security policy and potentially avoid lawsuits or regulatory audits.

In the US., there are two primary areas of legal governance affecting cybersecurity actions related to the collection of network data: (1) authority to monitor and collect the data and (2) the admissibility of the collection methods. There are three areas of law related to computer security that are important to know about. The first is found in the United States Constitution. The Fourth Amendment allows for protection against unreasonable search and seizure. The Fifth Amendment allows for protection against self-incrimination. Although the amendments were written before there were problems caused by people misusing computers, the principles in them apply to how computer forensics is practiced.

Second, anyone concerned with computer forensics must know how three US Statutory laws affect them. The text of these laws can be found at the US Department of Justice website. They are summarized in Appendix B. Violations of any one of these statutes during the practice of computer forensics could constitute a federal felony punishable by a fine and/or imprisonment. It is always advisable to consult your legal counsel if you are in doubt about the implications of any computer forensics action on behalf of your organization.

Third, the US Federal rules of evidence about hearsay, authentication, reliability, and best evidence must be understood.

Of the three areas above, the US Constitution and US Statutory Laws primarily govern the collection process, while the Federal Rules of Evidence deal mostly with admissibility in court.

If system administrators possess the technical skills and ability to preserve critical information related to a suspected security incident in a forensically sound manner and are aware of the legal issues related to forensics, they will be a great asset to their organization. Should an intrusion lead to a court case, the organization with computer forensics capability will be at a distinct advantage. With people spending an increasing amount of time using mobile devices, computers, and networks, there are bound to be more alibis that depend on digital evidence. Digital evidence will rarely

© View Apart/Shutterstock.com

show that someone was at a specific location at a specific time; however, it can show that the device was at that location. Through the use of other supporting evidence, such as a phone call in progress or an e-mail sent, the device can be associated with an individual.

REGULATING THE INTERNET: THE GOOD, THE BAD, AND THE UGLY

On 15 March 2015, the Federal Communications Commission (FCC) finally issued a ruling intended to ensure a free and open Internet was sustained. However, as with all government regulation, there is good in FCC Order 15-24; there is also bad; and most importantly, there is some real concern about the ugliness that underlies the way it was ultimately consolidated and released. Let's start by looking at some of the good that is contained within the Order.

To paraphrase Commissioner Wheeler's appended statement to the Order, the Internet and therefore Broadband networks must be fast, fair, and open. We agree with this perspective and so should you. This is something that we all want to see maintained. These three components are essential to the continued innovation and opportunity the Internet offers to everybody from startup businesses to free speech advocates. The Order established three rules intended to maintain these fundamental concepts.

> Para. 112—the No Blocking Rule: *A person engaged in the provision of broadband Internet access service, insofar as such person is so engaged, shall not block lawful content, applications, services, or nonharmful [sic] devices, subject to reasonable network management.*

> Para. 119—the No Throttling Rule: *A person engaged in the provision of broadband Internet access service, insofar as such person is so engaged, shall not impair or degrade lawful Internet traffic on the basis of Internet content, application, or service, or use of a non-harmful device, subject to reasonable network management.*

> Para. 125—the No Paid Prioritization Rule: *A person engaged in the provision of broadband Internet access service, insofar as such person is so engaged, shall not engage in paid prioritization. "Paid prioritization" refers to the management of a broadband provider's network to directly or indirectly favor some traffic over other traffic, including through use of techniques such as traffic shaping, prioritization, resource reservation, or other forms of preferential traffic management, either (a) in exchange for consideration (monetary or otherwise) from a third party, or (b) to benefit an affiliated entity.*

If this were where the rulemaking left off, rather than where it began, then establishing rules for the Internet would make sense. Unfortunately, the FCC went about establishing these rules by claiming potential threats and violations from all manner of beastly origins as their justification for moving forward—and moving beyond the fundamentals of Net Neutrality.

It is the fearmongering by the FCC in their order that drives the remainder of their actions. For example, Commissioner Clyburn delves into a terrifying potential apocalypse of which there is no reported evidence. Clyburn argues that without these rules any broadband provider could curtail free speech by throttling or blocking content, or through the extraction of restrictive tolls. This would reduce the Internet in the United States to a similarity with police states worldwide—where the service provider restricts speech and access based on their own concepts of acceptable content.

Commissioner Rosenworcel adds to the fearmongering in her succinct argument that:

> "We cannot have a two-tiered Internet with fast lanes that speed the traffic of the privileged and leave the rest of us lagging behind. We cannot have gatekeepers who tell us what we can and cannot do and where we can and cannot go online. And we do not need blocking, throttling, and paid prioritization schemes that undermine the Internet as we know it" (FCC 15-24, p. 320).

She's right! But there is no evidence this has happened or will happen.

In fact, I'd be happy to pay a bit more for faster service if my broadband provider offered that. We conduct research and writing using online assets and information sources. Sustained high-speed access is particularly important when we're conducting online courses or researching a topic. The throttling problem addressed in the FCC Order isn't the real problem. Instead, the order should have prohibited the throttling of information suppliers (which it does) while concurrently allowing a broadband provider to allow consumers to select their speed and pay an associated premium for faster connectivity. Unfortunately, it doesn't address or allow the later proposition.

Commissioner Pai writes that this Order will result in higher costs, slower service, stifle competition, particularly resulting in the loss of small competitors in the rural arena. He's right in that the burden of complying with Title II regulations and micromanagement could wipe out many small businesses through being taxed as telecommunications providers. That the majority in this 3–2 FCC decision based their argument on the application of Title II to Broadband providers as essential to prevent a hypothetical list of problems that have few real examples to fall upon is just plain ludicrous.

The Order specifically defines broadband Internet access service as:

> *A mass-market retail service by wire or radio that provides the capability to transmit data to and receive data from all or substantially all Internet endpoints, including any capabilities that are incidental to and enable the operation of the communications service, but excluding dial-up Internet access service. This term also encompasses any service that the Commission finds to be providing a functional equivalent of the service described in the previous sentence, or that is used to evade the protections set forth in this Part.* (FCC 15-24, p. 10)

It goes on to apply Title II to BOTH fixed and mobile broadband providers (FCC 15-24, 14, 15, & 22).

Pai states that, "Title II is not just a solution in search of a problem—it's a government solution that creates a real-world problem" (FCC 15-24, 334). There are many faults in the rulemaking process where the rules proposed in the 2014 Notice of Proposed Rule Making (NPRM 14-28) differ from the final rules adopted in the current FCC Order. Pai attacks the very premise that the FCC has the authority to reclassify broadband providers and mobile broadband as a Title II telecommunications service, essentially utilizing his dissent as a forum for building an evidentiary case for future court challenges to this Order.

Commissioner Pai's dissent aggressively charges what is clearly stated within the order—the forbearance on Universal Service Fees is only temporary. You know what USFs are—they are the charges that make having a telephone more expensive than using the telephone. USF will ultimately be applied to broadband providers and consumer costs will rise. When it comes to this new Order addressing broadband, Pai writes, "More new taxes are coming. It is just a matter of when" (FCC 15-24, 326). With FCC Order 15-22 the stage is set for the imposition of user fees, access fees, local, state, and federal communications taxes, etc. It's just a matter of time—and we don't know how long it will be before these get implemented. The forbearance of these is always left open-ended. They could be implemented tomorrow, next month, or just prior to the next election cycle—whenever it is most expedient for the government to do so.

Now for the ugly that you've all been waiting for. The application of Title II status to fixed and mobile broadband providers making them regulated common carriage systems is a direct refutation of decades of FCC rulemaking and Congressional legislation. That it originated as an afterthought in the 2014 NPRM as a point for future discussion is instructive.

Commissioner O'Rielly notes in the opening of his dissent that the application of Title II has been intentionally hidden from public view and imposed without sufficient consideration, saying,

> "It is fauxbearance: all of Title II applied through the backdoor of sections 201 and 202 of the Act, and section 706 of the 1996 Act. Moreover, all of it is premised on a mythical 'virtuous cycle'—not actual harms to edge providers or consumers" (FCC 15-24, 385).

Seems like there is some dissention within the ranks when it comes to how Title II was applied to the Internet.

When President Obama made it a clear component of what his plans were for regulating the Internet—the process at the FCC suddenly went underground. The White House never released its regulation plan for the Internet, but provided it in secret to only a select few of the FCC hierarchy. That plan still has never been released for public scrutiny. Yet in March 2015 we suddenly saw the FCC Chairman and the Commissioners supported by Democrats in Congress endorsing a complete government take-over of the Internet through application of Title II? If this doesn't scare you—it should.

The simplest expression of what all this really means comes from Commissioner Pai who notes,

> "I am optimistic that we will look back on today's vote as an aberration, a temporary deviation from the bipartisan path that has served us so well. I don't know whether this plan will be vacated by a court, reversed by Congress, or overturned by a future Commission. But I do believe that its days are numbered." (FCC 15-24, 384).

As of the writing of this book, there has been absolutely no movement to overturn the FCC Order.

We've read all 400 pages of the FCC Order, including all the footnotes. We've even gone back to review the 2014 NPRM that started this process, the Verizon court case, etc. This FCC Order scares the authors of this text. It places control of the Internet in the US one step away from the same control exercised by China and Saudi Arabia over the people's access to information in those countries.

CONCLUSION

Preventing, identifying, and punishing cybercrime is essential to maintaining security. This is true of organizations at all levels. However sensitive a situation may be, the rights of all involved must be protected. Sometimes an apparent perpetrator may be innocent. Certainly, most accused will offer an alibi. It must be acknowledged that actions in one country may be legal, but in another nation those very same actions may fail legal scrutiny. Knowledge of your legal environment is critical and then it may not be enough.

QUESTIONS FOR FURTHER CONSIDERATION

1. How can you identify laws, either local or national that affect you?

2. Laws gain strength by being referenced in other laws; how might this affect laws that deal with the Internet or Intellectual Property?

3. Could traditional laws be interpreted as applying to the Internet? If so, how?

4. Could contract law be referenced when referring to Internet transactions? To your knowledge has this occurred? Is it foreseeable?

5. How do standard transactions on the Internet vary from short-term contracts? Are they contracts?

REFERENCES

18 U.S. Code § 1030—Fraud and Related Activity in Connection with Computers

The Cybercrime Convention Committee (T-Cy), 26 March 2008. "Cybercrime" Provisions In The Council Of Europe Convention On The Protection Of Children Against Sexual Exploitation And Sexual Abuse, T-CY (2008) 01. Council of Europe. http://www.coe.int/t/dg1/legalcooperation/economiccrime/cybercrime/T-CY/T-CY%20(2008)%2003%20E%20-%20Sexual%20exploitation%20of%20children.PDF

Government reading room web site http://www.us-cert.gov/reading_room/forensics.pdf, produced 2008 by US-CERT, a government organization. Updated 2008.

Tony Bradley, CISSP-ISSAP. 20 October 2016. Host-Based Intrusion Protection: Things to look for in this last line of defense. Lifewire. Available at: https://www.lifewire.com/host-based-intrusion-prevention-2486685.

Trujillo, Mario. 2014. "Dems to FCC: 'Time for action' on Web reclassification." The Hill (Dec. 18). http://bit.ly/1GwPOTF.

Wheeler, Tom. 2015. "FCC Chairman Tom Wheeler: This Is How We Will Ensure Net Neutrality." *Wired* (Feb. 4). http://wrd.cm/1EGifR4.

The White House. 2014. "Net Neutrality: President Obama's Plan for a Free and Open Internet" (Nov. 10). http://www.whitehouse.gov/net-neutrality.

CHAPTER 12

"HONEY, DID YOU LOCK THE INTERNET?"

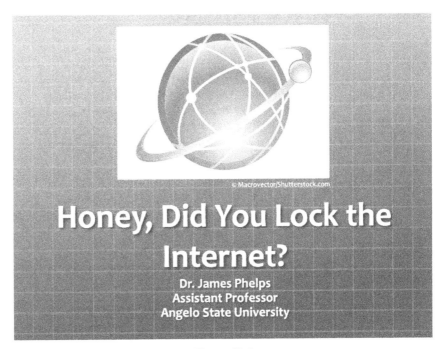

Figure 12.1

KEY WORDS

Avalanche	Identity Theft	SETI@home
Cyberspace	Ransomware	Silk Road

IT'S TIME TO LOCK YOUR INTERNET

In 2013 the US took down the online narcotics-selling Tor network, "**Silk Road**." At the end of 2016 thirty-nine countries combined efforts and took down the "**Avalanche**" criminal network, blocking more than 800,000 malicious domains and seizing servers in over forty international jurisdictions. While shutting down Avalanche will produce a temporary slowdown in the distribution of malware and **ransomware**, just like the removal of Silk Road in 2013, there will be many more networks that will replace the original ones.

SILK ROAD
An online narcotics-selling Tor network taken down by the US in 2013.

AVALANCHE
Criminal network taken down at the end of 2016.

RANSOMWARE
Malicious software inadvertently downloaded to a computer that subsequently locks the computer screen until an acceptable pass code is entered, usually after some sort of money transfer.

Cybersecurity is an interesting issue for all of us. One of the questions we face is who is ultimately responsible for protecting us from the never-ending crime spree to which constant connectivity exposes us? We propose that the answer is you!

In 2014 Dr. Phelps presented an informational lecture on the importance of cybersecurity to the San Angelo Texas Rotary Club; a business group. The audience consisted of small business owners that were faced with the same cyber threats that exist today. The concepts in this presentation were persistent in their applicability so we have decided to continue that trend.

WE LOCK EVERYTHING

It seems that today we lock everything. We lock the doors and windows. We keep our offices locked. We put child safety locks on ground level cabinets. We install trigger locks on our firearms. We even have time-out locks on our mobile phones. Why?

Primarily, we lock everything to prevent others from accessing whatever is inside. Not because we are paranoid, or feel threatened, or even feel

vulnerable. We lock ourselves in, and others out to offer a sense of individual and corporate security. We all know that these locks are essentially
meaningless to the truly intent and dedicated people that want access. Yet
we still take the time, effort, and expense out of a need for a feeling of safety
and security, or in some cases because the law requires us to do so.

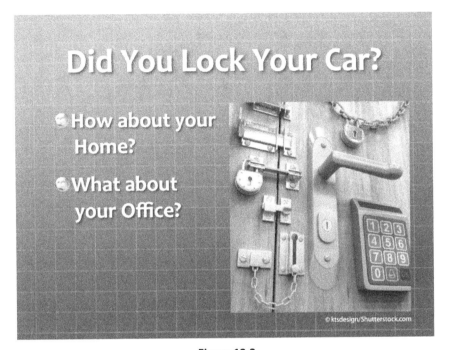

Figure 12.2

Yet we keep some items more secure and safe than others. Consider the
typical American automobile garage. What is inside? Your gym equipment,
bicycles, snow skies, some tools, perhaps a shelf or two with paint cans that
are so old you can't remember in which room the paint was used. Maybe
you have a workbench or two. Some power tools or lawn equipment and
of course, the garbage cans. We might even have a couple 4-wheeler toys
sitting in there, or perhaps that rare 1961 Harley Shovel-Head, back behind
all the cardboard boxes with the unpacked "things" from the last two or
three moves. If you are like most Americans, you can't get your vehicles
into the garage.

What we don't do is put our $50,000 pick-up truck into the garage. We
leave the truck exposed to the elements, subjected to hail, wind, snow,
and ice; not even covered to protect it from the UV damage from the sun.
Easily reachable by local hoodlums that want to spray paint or scratch

the doors and sidewalls. With single locks on the doors that are easy to "jimmy" open. Only a simple alarm system may exist to even notify you that somebody busted into the vehicle. You may not even have the alarm set most days and not even know! In fact, you locked and set the alarm but when you took the keys out of your pocket you accidently pushed the unlock button and didn't know (I did that once and had lots stolen that night). Yet, how much safer would that truck be if you put it inside the garage and closed the door? Not really all that much more protection – but perhaps a significant effort to put the most valuable item you own outside of the house itself behind the equivalent of a firewall.

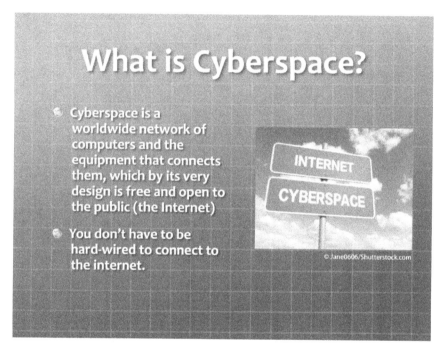

Figure 12.3

CYBERSPACE
A worldwide network of computers and the equipment that connects them, which by its very design is free and open to the public.

The devices we use to connect to **cyberspace** are much like our pick-up truck that is parked outside of the garage. We frequently fail to ensure that we have them sufficiently protected from intrusion, theft, and damage. This is why we need to understand the threats we are subject to and the means available to protect us.

NOT GETTING BURNED

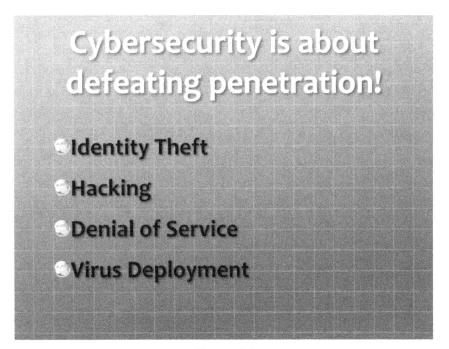

Figure 12.4

IDENTITY THEFT
When someone appropriates another's personal information without their knowledge to commit theft or fraud.

The primary threats we see are **identity thef**t, hacking, denial of service, and the viruses and malware that get inside our systems. How we identify these and recognize them for what they are is important not just from the perspective of IT staff, but from the viewpoint of management that has to deal with the rest of an organization's employees. Ensuring that you are effectively teaching others what to look for, how to identify something that is wrong, and what to do next is important for everybody.

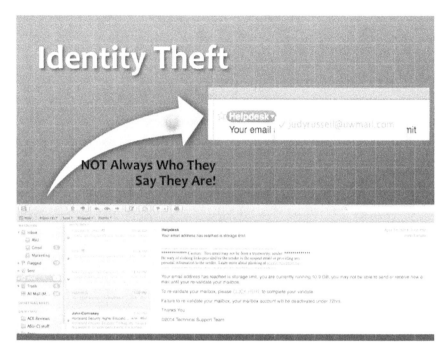

Figure 12.5

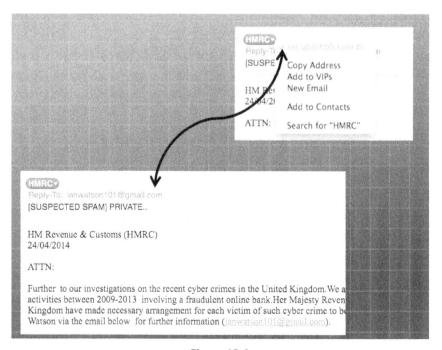

Figure 12.6

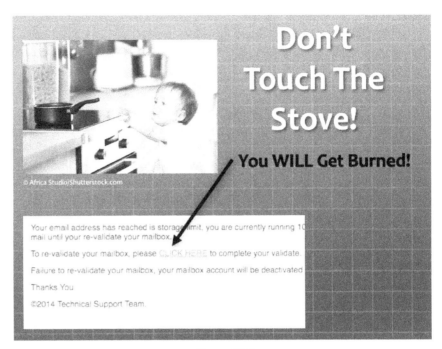

Figure 12.7

Just as we don't want children touching hot pots on a stove, we don't want our employees and co-workers clicking on a link that might infect our entire system. None of us want to deal with the issues of SPAM, spoofing, and the like. Even more than that we don't want to deal with malware and ransomware getting into our systems. To accomplish this means of protection within your organization requires you to be always aware of the latest and greatest scams and hacks so that you can address the problems through upgrades to your system, while concurrently educating your workforce on these without constantly dumping masses of new information on them and creating a situation where they are no longer paying attention.

Figure 12.8

WHO IS USING YOUR WIFI?

Stanley Konter, CEO of Savannah's Sabre Technologies, said, "The problem has gotten more prevalent with always-on, high-speed internet access. Attackers are always out there looking for that type of computer." What Konter is referring to is the fact that whenever your computer, cell phone, tablet, or credit card is connected to the Internet, that connection goes both ways and when the computer is always on and always connected, it becomes an available target for those wanting to use it, not just to get your information, but to establish a bot they can use down the road. Once somebody has a backdoor to your device, they have the ability to create a bot and attach it to a net. This gives them the power of your device, along with all the other devices, and that creates a multiplier of capability only limited by the processing capacity of the whole.

Figure 12.9

SETI
Search for Extra-Terrestrial Intelligence.

One of the first botnets ever created was done so with the intent of accomplishing good, not evil. The Search for Extra-Terrestrial Intelligence (SETI) created a software program called **SETI@home**. It took the multiplier effect of a botnet and determined that if the computers were always on, always connected, why not use their down time to process masses of data collected from the constant scan of space. Finding triplets in the data created maps of locations in the sky where we might want to look more closely for transmissions from other intelligent beings. The concept was excellent. So good that others thought that this same method might be appropriate for conducting other operations.

ATTACK OF THE BOTNETS

This is where the world has come, from botnets being used for science to similar networks being used for warfare—of a sort. It is possible to attack and not damage. This happened with Dyn on October, 21, 2016, when a DDOS attack from tens of millions of discrete IP addresses associated with the Mirai botnet among others overwhelmed the Dyn system with requests, preventing access to such popular services as Twitter.

The problem today is that there are an uncountable number of items that connect to the Internet through hard and wireless links. Each of these can be and have been corrupted with malware that can be triggered to do something we would normally consider improbable, but not impossible. The attack on Dyn is a clear example that such systems are not only in place, but capable of overwhelming even major companies. The Internet of Things (IoT) is here to stay—the question to ask is if your Things are being used by somebody else. Imagine if the same attack that hit Dyn was used to strike at the Department of Homeland Security websites. Or perhaps the Department of Justice or the Federal Aviation Administration. What would such an outage as happened with Twitter do to the aircraft control systems across the US or Europe? Would your organization carry some culpability or liability for another person using your Things to attack another party? How would you know? Here is where specialized legal advice might come in handy. So too would taking steps to ensure that all those Things around the office and home are actually secure.

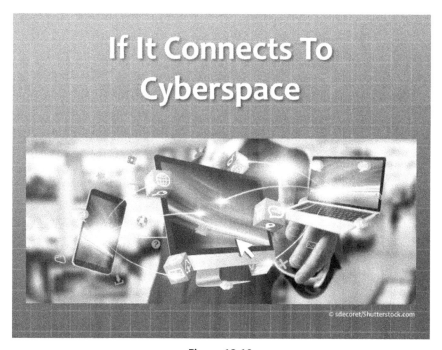

Figure 12.10

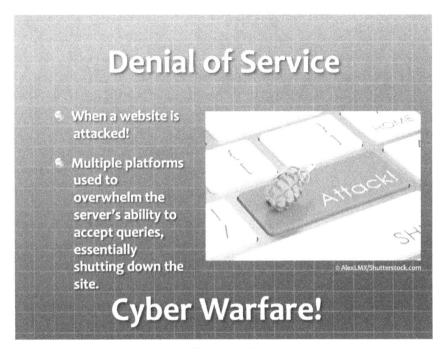

Figure 12.11

We have to go out of our way to constantly update and educate people about the reality of a constantly evolving threat matrix. Cybersecurity is not a one-time training session. Effective protection requires you to constantly work and upgrade systems, software, firewalls, backups, etc. It only takes one DDOS attack to bring down your entire network. The question you should be asking isn't, are we protected, but, how long will it take us to restore operations. When such an event happens, we can watch it real-time, or after the fact, to study the impact and effects as well as the origins.

Among the companies that provide this information are Prolexic, a subsidiary of Akamai, available at: https://www.akamai.com/us/en/cloud-security.jsp.[1] Another is the Digital Attack Map, by Arbor Networks, Inc., showing real-time Internet usage with regions and a historical timeline allowing you to look back at previous events and study where they originated. This system allows real access to look at several attacks as they happened. It is available at: http://www.digitalattackmap.com. If you want an eye-opening experience, move the timeline bar to some point with high activity and hit the play button.

1. Of course, the authors are not endorsing any particular company or service, just sharing with our readers some interesting information they might be able to use when conducting training for their organizations.

WANTING TO CRY

To repeat ourselves, cybersecurity is not a one-time training session. This was clearly demonstrated on Friday, 12 May 2017, when a new version of an old cyber threat began appearing around the world. The first major impact was the National Health Service of Great Britain being forced to shut down all clinics, appointments, surgeries, and even ambulance service. This new threat was called WANNACRY and used the WANACRYPT0R worm to not only infect the initial computer, but to spread and encrypt files on other computers within the entire system. Fundamentally, WANNACRY was a combination of the typical ransomware and a self-propagating worm. The result was hundreds of thousands of known instances where computers were encrypted and locked in over 140 countries.

According to Andy Greenberg of *WIRED Magazine,* pieces of the encryption code within WANNACRY are potentially from earlier versions of similar software used to attack Sony Pictures in 2014 in retaliation for an anti-North Korean movie they were going to release, and to a recent attack on "the SWIFT banking system, netting tens of millions of dollars from Bangladeshi and Vietnamese banks" by a group known as Lazarus. While Lazarus is tied to the North Korean government, it's important to note that as of this writing neither Symantec nor Kaspersky labs have stated the current WANNACRY ransomware is also connected. Interestingly, Greenberg also notes that a portion of the virus was also lifted "from an NSA exploit known as EternalBlue that a hacker group known as Shadow Brokers made public." It is important to note that this ransomware isn't up to the usual quality product employed by Lazarus and appears shoddy, even botching the payment programming.

The initial attack consisted of three versions designed to use a customized AES-256 cipher to corrupt text, images, audio, video, presentations, spreadsheets, and databases stored on the compromised device; targeting over 166 file types. It was stopped by a cybersecurity blogger who noticed in the code that there was an unregistered IP address being used to route the virus' communications. He, for only about $10, registered the IP address as his own and the spread of the virus immediately came to a halt. Of course, this was only a temporary fix as the originators of the virus could simply change that single part of the routing code and the virus would again begin to spread, freezing more computers. However, a week after the temporary fix, the hackers had yet to release a fourth version.

One new point that these hackers employed was to receive the ransom payment in Bitcoin, an untraceable digital (crypto-)currency. The amount of Bitcoin equaled $300. Of course, there was no guarantee that the hackers would unlock your files, nor that the virus would be removed. It was a pay the criminal and take your chances conundrum. Even if you did pay and your files were decrypted—the virus left a backdoor into your system that the hackers could later exploit. The encryption was of such a nature that encrypted files couldn't be unencrypted without the private key. So, your data was gone, even though it was still on your computer. To fix your problem without paying you had to erase your drive(s) where the files were encrypted, and rebuild them from off-site (external) storage. More importantly, you had to revert to stored versions that were created before the device was infected as its worm function could have compromised externally stored documents as well.

US-CERT did release an alert on the virus when it first appeared and later came out with a fact sheet concerning corrective actions you could take if you were targeted. This information is contained in the box following. As you can see, knowing how to talk to your cyber technicians and comprehend what they are telling you is an important skill. In this short section dealing with WANNACRY we have seen the need to understand AES, 256 byte encryption, worms, ransomware, external storage, IP addresses, cryptocurrency, and the US-CERT organization.

WHAT IS WANNACRY/WANACRYPTOR?

WannaCry is ransomware that contains a worm component. It attempts to exploit vulnerabilities in the Windows SMBv1 server to remotely compromise systems, encrypt their files, and spread to other hosts. Systems that have installed the MS17-010 patch are not vulnerable to the exploits used. Patches to address the vulnerabilities identified in Microsoft Security Bulletin MS17-010 are available for all versions of Windows from XP onward.

What if I have been infected?

▶ Isolate the system to prevent the malware from compromising additional devices.

  ▪ While the system may still be used, WannaCry will continue to encrypt files and attempt to spread.

▶ Do not connect to, or power on unpatched systems on, compromised networks.

▶ A cyber security incident can be reported to the NCCIC 24/7/365 at NCCICCustomerService@hq.dhs.gov or (888) 282-0870.

▶ Restore from backups. Encrypted files cannot currently be decrypted without the corresponding private key.

  ▪ If backups are not available, consider storing the encrypted data before wiping the computer in the event that a decryption method is found in the future.

What if a system cannot (currently) be patched?

There are several workarounds that can help protect systems from infection, including the following:

▶ Disable SMBv1 on every system connected to that network.

  ▪ https://support.microsoft.com/en-us/help/2696547/how-to-enable-and-disable-smbv1,-smbv2,-and-smbv3-in-windows-vista,-windows-server-2008,-windows-7,-windows-server-2008-r2,-windows-8,-and-windows-server-2012.

  ▪ While many modern devices will operate correctly without SMBv1, some older devices may experience communication or file/device access disruptions.

Source: http://www.us-cert.gov, May 12, 2017 by United States Computer Emergency Readiness Team (US-CERT), a division of The Department of Homeland Security.

> ▶ Block port 445 (Samba).
>
>> ▪ This may cause disruptions on systems that require port 445.
>
> ▶ Identify SMBv1 network traffic for investigation and mitigation.
>
>> ▪ Microsoft has useful information to help detect SMBv1 network traffic: https://blogs.technet.microsoft.com/ralphkyttle/2017/05/13/smb1-audit-active-usage-using-message-analyzer/.
>
> ▶ Vulnerable embedded systems that cannot be patched should be isolated or protected from potential network exploitation.

How do I decrypt my files?

> ▶ There is currently no method of decrypting encrypted files without having the private key.
>
> ▶ Paying the ransom does not guarantee that encrypted files will be restored. According to reporting, a backdoor remains after payment.

If I think a device is vulnerable and would like to report it, who do I contact?

> ▶ Contact ICS-CERT to report the issue at ics-cert@hq.dhs.gov or (877) 776-7585.

What else can I do going forward to prevent this kind of attack?

> ▶ Keep systems up to date and patch as soon as possible.
>
>> ▪ The CVEs for the vulnerabilities associated with WannaCry exploits are as follows: CVE-2017-0143, CVE-2017-0144, CVE-2017-0145, CVE-2017-0146, CVE-2017-0147, and CVE-2017-0148.
>
> ▶ Segregate networks based on functionality and the need to access resources.
>
> ▶ Keep offline data backups up to date.
>
> ▶ For additional information, reference ICS-CERT's Destructive Malware whitepaper.

National Cybersecurity and Communications Integration Center

Full Release Available at:
https://www.us-cert.gov/ncas/current-activity/2017/05/12/Multiple-Ransomware-Infections-Reported

THE NEXT-DOOR NEIGHBOR

We didn't start out thinking of hackers as bad people. In fact, the pioneers of the modern computing world were essentially hackers, those people that hacked out computer code to resolve interesting problems that others had yet to conceive existed. These people were looking for new ways to expand the potential of computer technology and associated operating systems by determining the way those systems functioned and inserting code to make them work in different, often better ways.

The most common trait found in hackers is curiosity to the point of obsession. Not only do hackers try to create ways to get inside software, in the process they often create software themselves. In some systems where the user can write code to the operating system, the very success of the process is dependent on hackers. So too are the patches that are inserted into code to accomplish fixes to systems. Not all hackers are out to rule the world, start a nuclear war, or steal the passwords to your daughter's online diary, but some are.

Figure 12.12

Unfortunately, not all hacking is benign. There are those whose intentions are not based on curiosity, but on a desire to corrupt, steal, compromise, or just be malicious in their actions. Whether a state actor, such as North Korea hacking into the Sony system to stop the distribution of a politically incorrect film about their Great Leader, or an Edward Snowden stealing information to expose secret government programs, these hackers give the rest a really bad name. They also are one of the greatest threats to our independence, the functioning of government, and the security of our financial institutions.

If it had been your bank and not one in South Africa that had tens of billions of dollars stolen from it, would your bank still be in business? If your public water supply system was susceptible to being hacked would you feel safe with twelve to fourteen tons of chlorine gas a couple blocks from your home? If the metro-rail system was vulnerable to outside manipulation of speed control and line switching would you ride it tomorrow? This is the problem we all must face every day—did the hackers get into a system I depend upon while I was sleeping last night? Does that super smart kid next door, the computer geek that comes over to help you watch movies without paying for the service, comprehend what he is doing when he zeros out his parent's water meter so they don't have to pay the bill for refilling the swimming pool?

Cybersecurity is a lot like sex. It can be fun, educational, and exciting. And without protection can lead to unwanted consequences.

A Little Pregnant!

- The Internet and Sex have a lot in common:
- Educational
- Exciting
- Fun
- And without protection – can lead to unwanted consequences, including diseases that never ever go away, and sometimes result in death.

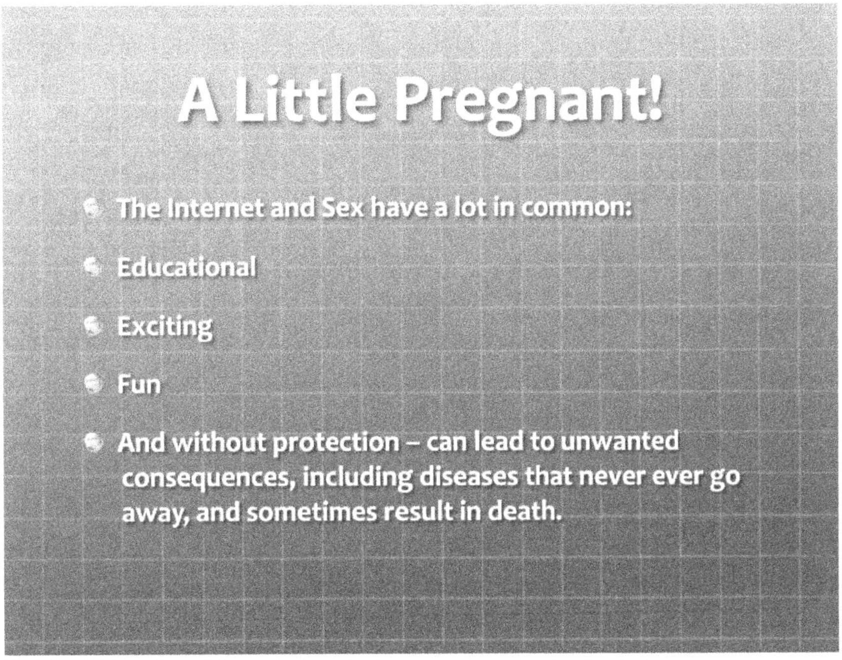

Figure 12.13

CONCLUSION

The problem with cyber systems is people. It is up to us, as the manager, owner, operator, or technician to understand what is happening and where those actions can take us. Access to the Internet is no longer a luxury, it is a necessity. Soon we will do everything with that smartphone, eliminating the need for credit/debit cards, and even cash. Prostitutes in some countries already carry card readers they operate through their cell phones so even illicit sex no longer requires cash, and is safer for the prostitute.

The cyber world is the future and either we can go completely off-line and become mountain hermits living in bunkers and reading old-fashioned print books by gas lamps—or we can take charge of our own security and embrace the future that is coming whether we want it to arrive or not. I happen to live in a hotel, in Dubai, next to the largest Chinese market outside of China. Walking around the shops and alcoves I see every imaginable new cyber and security invention possible, constantly being updated and changed as demand drives supply. I see every type of drone that is produced, every computer game, every electronic kitchen device, even computerized bathroom fittings. Believe me when I say that the future is already here and it won't be long before a HAL 9000 or Cyberdyne Systems run our daily lives through SKYNET.

Just as you wouldn't expect a fireman to show up to fight a fire without protection, so too should you think about the Internet and cybersecurity. Learn how to talk to those folks in IT. Understanding their language is essential to understanding your vulnerabilities and therefore knowing what the next step is to address those issues that threaten your organizations.

QUESTIONS FOR FURTHER CONSIDERATION

1. What would an outage as happened with Twitter in December 2016 do to the aircraft control systems across the US or Europe? Or are those systems so robust that such an attack would have no impact?

2. Would your organization carry some culpability or liability for another person using your Internet connected Things to attack another party? How would you know?

3. Having completed this book, are you better able to talk with your IT security professionals? If so, how? If not, what could we have done better?

REFERENCES

Akamai Technologies. 2016. https://www.akamai.com/us/en/cloud-security.jsp#DDOSAction.

Arbor Networks Inc. Digital Attack Map. Global DDOS attack data. http://www.digitalattackmap.com/#anim=1&color=0&country=ALL&list=0&time=17052&view=map.

Clarke, Arthur C. *2001 A Space Odyssey*. HAL 9000. A fictional computer character. https://en.wikipedia.org/wiki/HAL_9000.

Dynamic Network Services, Inc. 2016. http://dyn.com/blog/dyn-statement-on-10212016-ddos-attack/.

Fandom, powered by Wikia, Inc. 2016. http://terminator.wikia.com/wiki/Cyberdyne_Systems.

GoldSparrow. WannaCryptor or WanaCrypt0r Ransomware. 2017. Enigma Software Group, USA. https://www.enigmasoftware.com/wannacryptorransomware-removal/

Greenberg, A. 2017. The wannacryransomware has a link to suspected North Korean hackers. *Wired* (15 May). https://www.wired.com/2017/05/wannacry-ransomware-link-suspected-north-korean-hackers/

SETI@home. University of California at Berkeley. https://setiathome.berkeley.edu.

APPENDIX A

ACRONYMS

ACL	Access Control Lists
AES	Advanced Encryption Standard
AI	Artificial Intelligence
AKA	Also Known As
ALM	Avid Life Media
API	Application Programming Interface
APP	Application
ARPANET	Advanced Research Projects Agency Network
ATM	Automated Teller Machine
AT&T	American Telephone and Telegraph
Bytes	Binary Digits
CA	Certification Authority
CAN	Campus Area Network
CAN-SPAM	Controlling the Assault of Non-Solicited Pornography and Marketing Act
CCA	Chosen Ciphertext Attack
CCTV	Closed Circuit Television
CDA	Communications Decency Act
CEO	Chief Executive Officer
CFAA	Computer Fraud and Abuse Act
CIA	Confidentiality-Integrity-Availability Triad
CIO	Chief Information Officer
CIPA	Children's Internet Protection Act
CP	Cloud Provider

CPPA	Child Pornography Protection Act
CPU	Central Processing Unit
CRL	Certification Revocation List
CSA	Cloud Security Alliance
CSP	Cloud Service Provider
DARPA	Defense Advanced Research Projects Agency
DBMS	Database Management System
DDOS	Distributed Denial of Service
DEA	Data Encryption Algorithm
DES	Data Encryption Standard
DLP	Data Loss Prevention
DMCA	Digital Millennium Copyright Act
DMV	Department of Motor Vehicles
DNS	Domain Name System
DVR	Digital Video Recorder
ECC	Elliptical Curve Cryptography
ECPA	Electronic Communications Privacy Act
EITC	Emirates Integrated Telecommunications Company
EU	European Union
FBI	Federal Bureau of Investigation
FCC	Federal Communications Commission
FDIC	Federal Deposit Insurance Corporation
FE	Field Engineer
FedEx	Federal Express Corporation
FTP	File Transfer Protocol
GPU	Graphics Processing Unit
HTML	Hypertext Markup Language
HTTP	Hypertext Transfer Protocol
HTTPS	HTTP over SSL
IAM	Identity and Access Management
ICANN	Internet Corporation for Assigned Names and Numbers
IDS	Intrusion Detection System
IP	Internet Protocol
IPS	Intrusion Protection System
ISP	Internet Service Provider

IT	Information Technology
LAN	Local Area Network
LEO	Law Enforcement Officer
Mac	Macintosh Computer
MAC	Media Access Control
Malware	Malicious Software
MAN	Metropolis Area Network
MIME	Multi-Purpose Internet Mail Extensions
MTCN	Money Transfer Control Number
NAC	Network Access Control
NAS	Network Area Storage
NCSA	National Center for Supercomputing Applications
NIST	National Institute of Science and Technology
NRC	Nuclear Regulatory Commission
NSA	National Security Agency
OAEP	Optimal Asymmetric Encryption Padding
OS	Operating System
P2P	Peer to Peer
PAN	Personal Area Network
PC	Personal Computer
PGP	Pretty Good Protection
PIN	Personal Identification Number
PKI	Public Key Infrastructure
PRNG	Pseudorandom Number Generators
RAM	Random Access Memory
RFID	Radio Frequency Identification Chips
RIPE NCC	Reseaux IP Europeans Network Coordination Centre
RSA	Rivest-Shamir-Adleman scheme of encryption
S/MIME	Secure/Multipurpose Internet Mail Extensions
SAML	Security Assertion Markup Language
SANS	Storage Area Networks
SecaaS	Security as a Service
SEIM	Security Information and Event Management
SHA	Secure Hash Algorithm
SLA	Service Level Agreement

SOAP	Simple Object Access Protocol
SPAM	Solicited Pornography and Marketing
SPI	Serial Peripheral Interface
SSH	Secure Shell
SSL	Secure Socket Layer
SSO	Single Sign-On
SOW	Statement of Work
SQL	Structured Query Language
TCP	Transmission Control Protocol
TLS	Transport Layer Security
TOC	Technical Operations Center
Tor	The Onion Router
TRNG	True Random Number Generators
UAE	United Arab Emirates
UK	United Kingdom
UPS	United Parcel Service
USAA	United Services Automobile Association
USB	Universal Serial Bus
USPS	United States Postal Service
U.S.	United States of America
VoIP	Voice over Internet Protocol
VPN	Virtual Private Network
WAN	Wide Area Network
WEP	Wired Equivalent Privacy
WPA	WiFi Protected Access
WWW	World Wide Web
XML	Extensible Markup Language

SELECTED US LAW RELATED TO CYBERSECURITY

ELECTRONIC COMMUNICATIONS PRIVACY ACT OF 1986 (ECPA), 18 U.S.C. § 2510-22.

Background. The Electronic Communications Privacy Act and the Stored Wire Electronic Communications Act are commonly referred together as the Electronic Communications Privacy Act (ECPA) of 1986. The ECPA updated the Federal Wiretap Act of 1968, which addressed interception of conversations using "hard" telephone lines, but did not apply to interception of computer and other digital and electronic communications. Several subsequent pieces of legislation, including The USA PATRIOT Act, clarify and update the ECPA to keep pace with the evolution of new communications technologies and methods, including easing restrictions on law enforcement access to stored communications in some cases.

General Provisions. The ECPA, as amended, protects wire, oral, and electronic communications while those communications are being made, are in transit, and when they are stored on computers. The Act applies to e-mail, telephone conversations, and data stored electronically.

Civil Rights and Civil Liberties. "The structure of the SCA reflects a series of classifications that indicate the drafters' judgments about what kinds of information implicate greater or lesser privacy interests. For example, the drafters saw greater privacy interests in the content of stored e-mails than in subscriber account information. Similarly, the drafters believed that computing services available 'to the public' required more strict [sic] regulation than services not available to the public . . . To protect the array of privacy interests identified by its drafters, the [Act] offers varying degrees of legal protection depending on the perceived importance of the privacy interest involved. Some information can be obtained from providers with a subpoena; other information requires a special court order; and still other information requires a search warrant. In addition, some types of legal process require notice to the subscriber, while other types do not."

The Act reflects a general approach of providing greater privacy protection for materials in which there are greater privacy interests. For a more in-depth analysis, U.S. Dept. of Justice, Searching and Seizing Computers and Obtaining Electronic Evidence In Criminal Investigations (2009), pp. 115–116, (287pp | 1.01mb | PDF).

Specific Provisions. The ECPA has three titles:

Title I of the ECPA, which is often referred to as the Wiretap Act, prohibits the intentional actual or attempted interception, use, disclosure, or "procure[ment] [of] any other person to intercept or endeavor to intercept any wire, oral, or electronic communication." Title I also prohibits the use of illegally obtained communications as evidence. 18 U.S.C. § 2515.

Exceptions. Title I provides exceptions for operators and service providers for uses "in the normal course of his employment while engaged in any activity which is a necessary incident to the rendition of his service" and for "persons authorized by law to intercept wire, oral, or electronic communications or to conduct electronic surveillance, as defined in section 101 of the Foreign Intelligence Surveillance Act (FISA) of 1978." 18 U.S.C. § 2511. It provides procedures for Federal, State, and other government officers to obtain judicial authorization for intercepting such communications, and regulates the use and disclosure of information obtained through authorized wiretapping. 18 U.S.C. § 2516-18. A judge may issue a warrant authorizing interception of communications for up to 30 days upon a showing of probable cause that the interception will reveal evidence that an individual is committing, has committed, or is about to commit a "particular offense" listed in § 2516. 18 U.S.C. § 2518.

Title II of the ECPA, which is called the Stored Communications Act (SCA), protects the privacy of the contents of files stored by service providers and of records held about the subscriber by service providers, such as subscriber name, billing records, or IP addresses. 18 U.S.C. §§ 2701-12.

Title III of the ECPA, which addresses pen register and trap and trace devices, requires government entities to obtain a court order authorizing the installation and use of a pen register (a device that captures the dialed numbers and related information to which outgoing calls or communications are made by the subject) and/or a trap and trace (a device that captures the numbers and related information from which incoming calls and communications coming to the subject have originated). No actual communications are intercepted by a pen register or trap and trace. The authorization order can be issued on the basis of certification by the applicant that the information likely to be obtained is relevant to an ongoing criminal investigation being conducted by the applicant's agency.

Amendments. The ECPA was significantly amended by the Communications Assistance to Law Enforcement Act (CALEA) in 1994, the USA PATRIOT Act in 2001, the USA PATRIOT reauthorization acts in 2006, and the FISA Amendments Act of 2008. Other acts have made specific amendments of lesser significance.

Last accessed from: https://it.ojp.gov/PrivacyLiberty/authorities/statutes/1285

47 U.S. CODE SUBCHAPTER I—INTERCEPTION OF DIGITAL AND OTHER COMMUNICATIONS

1001 Definitions: For purposes of this subchapter—

(1)   The terms defined in section 2510 of title 18 have, respectively, the meanings stated in that section.

(2)   The term "call-identifying information" means dialing or signaling information that identifies the origin, direction, destination, or termination of each communication generated or received by a subscriber by means of any equipment, facility, or service of a telecommunications carrier.

(3)   The term "Commission" means the Federal Communications Commission.

(4)   The term "electronic messaging services" means software-based services that enable the sharing of data, images, sound, writing, or other information among computing devices controlled by the senders or recipients of the messages.

(5)   The term "government" means the government of the United States and any agency or instrumentality thereof, the District of Columbia, any commonwealth, territory, or possession of the United States, and any State or political subdivision thereof authorized by law to conduct electronic surveillance.

(6)   The term "information services"—

(A)   means the offering of a capability for generating, acquiring, storing, transforming, processing, retrieving, utilizing, or making available information via telecommunications; and

(B)   includes—

(i)   a service that permits a customer to retrieve stored information from, or file information for storage in, information storage facilities;

(ii)   electronic publishing; and

(iii)   electronic messaging services; but

(C)   does not include any capability for a telecommunications carrier's internal management, control, or operation of its telecommunications network.

(7)   The term "telecommunications support services" means a product, software, or service used by a telecommunications carrier for the internal signaling or switching functions of its telecommunications network.

(8)   The term "telecommunications carrier"—

(A)   means a person or entity engaged in the transmission or switching of wire or electronic communications as a common carrier for hire; and

(B)   includes—

(i)   a person or entity engaged in providing commercial mobile service (as defined in section 332(d) of this title); or

(ii)   a person or entity engaged in providing wire or electronic communication switching or transmission service to the extent that the Commission finds that such service is a replacement for a substantial portion of the local telephone exchange service and that it is in the public interest to deem such a person or entity to be a telecommunications carrier for purposes of this subchapter; but

(C) does not include—

(i) persons or entities insofar as they are engaged in providing information services; and

(ii) any class or category of telecommunications carriers that the Commission exempts by rule after consultation with the Attorney General.

1002 Assistance Capability Requirements

(a) **Capability requirements** Except as provided in subsections (b), (c), and (d) of this section and sections 1007(a) and 1008(b) and (d) of this title, a telecommunications carrier shall ensure that its equipment, facilities, or services that provide a customer or subscriber with the ability to originate, terminate, or direct communications are capable of—

(1) expeditiously isolating and enabling the government, pursuant to a court order or other lawful authorization, to intercept, to the exclusion of any other communications, all wire and electronic communications carried by the carrier within a service area to or from equipment, facilities, or services of a subscriber of such carrier concurrently with their transmission to or from the subscriber's equipment, facility, or service, or at such later time as may be acceptable to the government;

(2) expeditiously isolating and enabling the government, pursuant to a court order or other lawful authorization, to access call-identifying information that is reasonably available to the carrier—

(A) before, during, or immediately after the transmission of a wire or electronic communication (or at such later time as may be acceptable to the government); and

(B) in a manner that allows it to be associated with the communication to which it pertains, except that, with regard to information acquired solely pursuant to the authority for pen registers and trap and trace devices (as defined in section 3127 of title 18), such call-identifying information shall not include any information that may disclose the physical location of the subscriber (except to the extent that the location may be determined from the telephone number);

(3) delivering intercepted communications and call-identifying information to the government, pursuant to a court order or other lawful authorization, in a format such that they may be transmitted by means of equipment, facilities, or services procured by the government to a location other than the premises of the carrier; and

(4) facilitating authorized communications interceptions and access to call-identifying information unobtrusively and with a minimum of interference with any subscriber's telecommunications service and in a manner that protects—

  (A) the privacy and security of communications and call-identifying information not authorized to be intercepted; and

  (B) information regarding the government's interception of communications and access to call-identifying information.

(b) **Limitations**

  (1) **Design of features and systems configurations** This subchapter does not authorize any law enforcement agency or officer—

    (A) to require any specific design of equipment, facilities, services, features, or system configurations to be adopted by any provider of a wire or electronic communication service, any manufacturer of telecommunications equipment, or any provider of telecommunications support services; or

    (B) to prohibit the adoption of any equipment, facility, service, or feature by any provider of a wire or electronic communication service, any manufacturer of telecommunications equipment, or any provider of telecommunications support services.

  (2) **Information services; private networks and interconnection services and facilities** The requirements of subsection (a) do not apply to—

    (A) information services; or

    (B) equipment, facilities, or services that support the transport or switching of communications for private networks or for the sole purpose of interconnecting telecommunications carriers.

(3)   Encryption

A telecommunications carrier shall not be responsible for decrypting, or ensuring the government's ability to decrypt, any communication encrypted by a subscriber or customer, unless the encryption was provided by the carrier and the carrier possesses the information necessary to decrypt the communication.

(c)   Emergency or exigent circumstances

In emergency or exigent circumstances (including those described in sections 2518(7) or (11)(b) and 3125 of title 18 and section 1805(e) of title 50), a carrier at its discretion may comply with subsection (a)(3) by allowing monitoring at its premises if that is the only means of accomplishing the interception or access.

(d)   Mobile service assistance requirements

A telecommunications carrier that is a provider of commercial mobile service (as defined in section 332(d) of this title) offering a feature or service that allows subscribers to redirect, hand off, or assign their wire or electronic communications to another service area or another service provider or to utilize facilities in another service area or of another service provider shall ensure that, when the carrier that had been providing assistance for the interception of wire or electronic communications or access to call-identifying information pursuant to a court order or lawful authorization no longer has access to the content of such communications or call-identifying information within the service area in which interception has been occurring as a result of the subscriber's use of such a feature or service, information is made available to the government (before, during, or immediately after the transfer of such communications) identifying the provider of a wire or electronic communication service that has acquired access to the communications.

1004—Systems Security and Integrity

A telecommunications carrier shall ensure that any interception of communications or access to call-identifying information effected within its switching premises can be activated only in accordance with a court order or other lawful authorization and with the affirmative intervention of an individual officer or employee of the carrier acting in accordance with regulations prescribed by the Commission.

1005–COOPERATION OF EQUIPMENT MANUFACTURERS AND PROVIDERS OF TELECOMMUNICATIONS SUPPORT SERVICES

(a) Consultation

A telecommunications carrier shall consult, as necessary, in a timely fashion with manufacturers of its telecommunications transmission and switching equipment and its providers of telecommunications support services for the purpose of ensuring that current and planned equipment, facilities, and services comply with the capability requirements of section 1002 of this title and the capacity requirements identified by the Attorney General under section 1003 of this title.

(b) Cooperation

Subject to sections 1003(e), 1007(a), and 1008(b) and (d) of this title, a manufacturer of telecommunications transmission or switching equipment and a provider of telecommunications support services shall, on a reasonably timely basis and at a reasonable charge, make available to the telecommunications carriers using its equipment, facilities, or services such features or modifications as are necessary to permit such carriers to comply with the capability requirements of section 1002 of this title and the capacity requirements identified by the Attorney General under section 1003 of this title.

1007—Enforcement Orders

(a) Grounds for issuance A court shall issue an order enforcing this subchapter under section 2522 of title 18 only if the court finds that—

(1) alternative technologies or capabilities or the facilities of another carrier are not reasonably available to law enforcement for implementing the interception of communications or access to call-identifying information; and

(2) compliance with the requirements of this subchapter is reasonably achievable through the application of available technology to the equipment, facility, or service at issue or would have been reasonably achievable if timely action had been taken.

(b) Time for compliance

Upon issuing an order enforcing this subchapter, the court shall specify a reasonable time and conditions for complying with its order, considering the good faith efforts to comply in a timely manner, any effect on the carrier's, manufacturer's, or service provider's ability to continue to do business, the degree of culpability or delay in undertaking efforts to comply, and such other matters as justice may require.

(c) Limitations An order enforcing this subchapter may not—

(1) require a telecommunications carrier to meet the Government's [1] demand for interception of communications and acquisition of call-identifying information to any extent in excess of the capacity for which the Attorney General has agreed to reimburse such carrier;

(2) require any telecommunications carrier to comply with assistance capability requirement [2] of section 1002 of this title if the Commission has determined (pursuant to section 1008(b)(1) of this title) that compliance is not reasonably achievable, unless the Attorney General has agreed (pursuant to section 1008(b)(2) of this title) to pay the costs described in section 1008(b)(2)(A) of this title; or

(3) require a telecommunications carrier to modify, for the purpose of complying with the assistance capability requirements of section 1002 of this title, any equipment, facility, or service deployed on or before January 1, 1995, unless—

(A) the Attorney General has agreed to pay the telecommunications carrier for all reasonable costs directly associated with modifications necessary to bring the equipment, facility, or service into compliance with those requirements; or

(B) the equipment, facility, or service has been replaced or significantly upgraded or otherwise undergoes major modification.

18 U.S. CODE § 2522—ENFORCEMENT OF THE COMMUNICATIONS ASSISTANCE FOR LAW ENFORCEMENT ACT

(a)   **Enforcement by Court Issuing Surveillance Order.—**

If a court authorizing an interception under this chapter, a State statute, or the Foreign Intelligence Surveillance Act of 1978 (50 U.S.C. 1801 et seq.) or authorizing use of a pen register or a trap and trace device under chapter 206 or a State statute finds that a telecommunications carrier has failed to comply with the requirements of the Communications Assistance for Law Enforcement Act, the court may, in accordance with section 108 of such Act, direct that the carrier comply forthwith and may direct that a provider of support services to the carrier or the manufacturer of the carrier's transmission or switching equipment furnish forthwith modifications necessary for the carrier to comply.

(b)   **Enforcement Upon Application by Attorney General.—**

The Attorney General may, in a civil action in the appropriate United States district court, obtain an order, in accordance with section 108 of the Communications Assistance for Law Enforcement Act, directing that a telecommunications carrier, a manufacturer of telecommunications transmission or switching equipment, or a provider of telecommunications support services comply with such Act.

(c)   **Civil Penalty.—**

(1)   **In general.—**

A court issuing an order under this section against a telecommunications carrier, a manufacturer of telecommunications transmission or switching equipment, or a provider of telecommunications support services may impose a civil penalty of up to $10,000 per day for each day in violation after the issuance of the order or after such future date as the court may specify.

(2)   **Considerations.—**In determining whether to impose a civil penalty and in determining its amount, the court shall take into account—

(A)   the nature, circumstances, and extent of the violation;

(B) the violator's ability to pay, the violator's good faith efforts to comply in a timely manner, any effect on the violator's ability to continue to do business, the degree of culpability, and the length of any delay in undertaking efforts to comply; and

(C) such other matters as justice may require.

(d) Definitions.—

As used in this section, the terms defined in section 102 of the Communications Assistance for Law Enforcement Act have the meanings provided, respectively, in such section.

GLOSSARY

Access: Ability to make use of any information system (IS) resource; ability and means to communicate with or otherwise interact with a system, to use system resources to handle information, to gain knowledge of the information the system contains, or to control system components and functions.

Access Control: The process of granting or denying specific requests to: (1) obtain and use information and related information processing services; and (2) enter specific facilities.

Access Control Lists (ACLs): A register of: (1) users (including groups, machines, processes) who have been given permission to use a particular system resource; and (2) the types of access they have been permitted.

Asset: People, property, and information.

Asymmetric Encryption: A form of encryption where keys come in pairs. . . . Frequently (but not necessarily), the keys are interchangeable, in the sense that if key A encrypts a message, then B can decrypt it, and if key B encrypts a message, then key A can decrypt it.

Asymmetries of power: The third vulnerability inherent in the Internet; with over three billion people connected, there is much room for those who want to interrupt service or attack corporations or governments.

Auction Fraud: Fraud attributable to the misrepresentation of a product advertised for sale through an Internet auction site or the non-delivery of products purchased through an Internet auction site.

Authentication: Verifying the identity of a user, process, or device, often as a prerequisite to allowing access to resources in an information system.

Availability: Ensuring timely and reliable access to and use of information.

Avalanche: Criminal network taken down at the end of 2016.

Backdoor: An undocumented way of gaining access to a computer system.

Bit Stream: Predetermined sized stream of data.

Blacklist: A list of discrete entities, such as hosts or applications, that have been previously determined to be associated with malicious activity.

Block Cipher: A method of encrypting text (to produce ciphertext) in which a cryptographic key and algorithm are applied to a block of data (for example, sixty-four contiguous bits) at once as a group rather than to one bit at a time.

Browser History: The list of web pages a user has visited recently—and associated data such as page title and time of visit—which is recorded by web browser software as standard for a certain period of time.

Bus Topology: A line between and connecting multiple machines.

CA/Browser Forum: The Certification Authority Browser Forum, a group comprised of the leading browser and Certification Authority companies.

Campus Area Network: A computer network made up of an interconnection of local area networks (LANs) within a limited geographical area.

CFAA: Fraud and related activity in connection with computers.

Chief Information Officer (CIO): Agency official responsible for: (1) providing advice or other assistance to the head of the executive agency and other senior management personnel of the agency to ensure that information systems are acquired and information resources are managed in a manner that is consistent with laws, Executive Orders, directives, policies, regulations, and priorities established by the head of the agency; (2) developing, maintaining, and facilitating the implementation of a sound and integrated information system architecture for the agency; and (3) promoting the effective and efficient design and operation of all major information resources management processes for the agency, including improvements to work processes of the agency.

Child Pornography: Realistic images representing a minor engaged in sexually explicit conduct.

Cipher Block: A method of encrypting text (to produce ciphertext) in which a cryptographic key and algorithm are applied to a block of data (for example, sixty-four contiguous bits) at once as a group rather than to one bit at a time; another way of saying Block Cipher.

Cipher Block Chaining: Mode of operation for a block cipher (one in which a sequence of bits are encrypted as a single unit or block with a cipher key applied to the entire block).

Cipher Text: The plaintext that has been changed, so that it is not easily distinguishable for people, to prevent unauthorized disclosure (providing us either security or privacy).

Client: A piece of computer hardware or software that accesses a service made available by a server.

Computer: Programmable, usually electronic device that can store, retrieve, and process data.

Computer forensics: The main purpose is to identify, collect, preserve, and analyze data in a way that preserves the integrity of the evidence collected so it can be used effectively in a legal case.

Confidentiality: Preserving authorized restrictions on access and disclosure, including means for protecting personal privacy and proprietary information.

Cyberspace: A worldwide network of computers and the equipment that connects them, which by its very design is free and open to the public.

Dark web: A subset of the deep web, which requires special software and/or authorization to access.

Data: A subset of information in an electronic format that allows it to be retrieved or transmitted.

Data at Rest: Data is being stored.

Data Block: The smallest unit of data used by a database.

Data Breech: An incident in which sensitive, protected, or confidential data has been viewed, stolen, or used by an individual unauthorized to do so.

Data Collection Requirements: A determination of the intelligence needed to perform organizational functions.

Data Protection: Securing data from unauthorized access.

Debt Elimination: Generally involve websites advertising a legal way to dispose of mortgage loans and credit card debts.

Deep web: Anything on the Internet which is not indexed by a search engine.

Encryption: When data is altered from its original form by use of cipher text: the process of changing plaintext into cipher text for the purpose of security or privacy.

Fabrication: Also known as counterfeiting. It bypasses authenticity checks, and essentially is mimicking or impersonating information.

FCC: Federal Communications Commission, which oversees telecommunications in the United States.

Field Engineer: Technician charged with design, implementation, support, and maintenance of the networks within their region.

File Encryption: Enables files to be transparently encrypted to protect confidential data from attackers with physical access to the computer.

Fraud: The act of using a computer to take or alter electronic data, or to gain unlawful use of a computer or system.

Full header: In e-mail messages, full headers contain the addresses of all the computer systems that have relayed a message in-between you and the message's sender.

Hardware: the electro-mechanical components and external attachments used to effectively connect operating systems.

Hashing: Comparing hash values from an original document versus a received document to provide an indication as to whether a document has been altered from its original state.

ICANN: The Internet Corporation for Assigned Names and Numbers, a nonprofit organization that primarily maintains the root DNS system.

Identity Theft: When someone appropriates another's personal information without their knowledge to commit theft or fraud.

Information: An instance of an information type, or any communication or representation of knowledge such as facts, data, or opinions in any medium or form, including textual, numerical, graphic, cartographic, narrative, or audiovisual.

Information Security: Protecting information and information systems from unauthorized access, use, disclosure, disruption, modification, or destruction.

Information Technology: Any equipment or interconnected system or subsystem of equipment that is used in the automatic acquisition, storage, manipulation, management, movement, control, display, switching, interchange, transmission, or reception of data or information by the executive agency. The term information technology includes computers, ancillary equipment, software, firmware and similar procedures, services (including support services), and related resources.

Integrity: Guarding against improper information modification or destruction, and includes ensuring information nonrepudiation and authenticity.

Interception: An attack on data in transit.

Internet Extortion: Hacking into and controlling various industry databases, promising to release control back to the company if funds are received, or the subjects are given web administrator jobs.

Internet of Things: Describes a recent trend to incorporate technology into nearly every aspect of our physical world.

Interruption: An attack on availability such as a denial of service attack (or DOS).

Intrusion Defense Systems: A device or software application that monitors a network or systems for malicious activity or policy violations.

Intrusion Prevention Systems: A network security/threat prevention technology that examines network traffic flows to detect and prevent vulnerability exploits.

Investment Fraud: An offer using false or fraudulent claims to solicit investments or loans, or providing for the purchase, use, or trade of forged or counterfeit securities.

IP addresses: The specific and unique numbers assigned to computers.

ISP: Internet Service Provider.

Jurisdiction: Where a crime takes place.

Lack of Borders: A vulnerability of the Internet; the web is globalized and this creates a major problem when a crime is committed, terrorists use the web, or nation-states launch cyber-attacks on other nation-states.

Local Area Network: A computer network that links devices within a building or group of adjacent buildings, especially one with a radius of less than 1 km.

Logical Network Topologies: The arrangement of devices on a computer network and how they communicate with one another.

Lotteries: Randomly contacting e-mail addresses advising them they have been selected as the winner of an international lottery.

Metropolitan Area Network: Is similar to a local area network (LAN) but spans an entire city or campus. MANs are formed by connecting multiple LANs.

Modification: An attack that tampers with a resource. Its aim is to modify information that is being communicated with two or more parties.

Network Vulnerabilities: A weakness which allows an attacker to reduce a system's information assurance. Vulnerability is the intersection of three elements: a system susceptibility or flaw, attacker access to the flaw, and attacker capability to exploit the flaw.

Networks: Information system(s) implemented with a collection of interconnected components. Such components may include routers, hubs, cabling, telecommunications controllers, key distribution centers, and technical control devices.

Nigerian Letter: The scam combines the threat of impersonation fraud with a variation of an advance fee scheme in which a letter, e-mail, or fax is received by the potential victim.

Non-Repudiation: Ability to determine who performs an action; assurance that the sender of information is provided with proof of delivery and the recipient is provided with proof of the sender's identity, so neither can later deny having processed the information.

On The Fly: Data in motion.

Onion Router: An overlay network that operates on the public web, which uses increasing layers of encryption to make end-to-end web traffic anonymous.

Patch Management: Planning the cycle of security updates to software.

Personal Area Network: A computer network used for data transmission amongst devices such as computers, telephones, tablets, and personal digital assistants.

Phishing: Forged or faked electronic documents intended to acquire personal information to commit another Internet crime.

Physical Network Topologies: The way that the devices on a network are arranged and how they communicate with each other.

Plain Text: Data as we would normally read it.

Ponzi/Pyramid: Investment scams in which investors are promised abnormally high profits on their investments.

Privacy: From a legal standpoint it is: the right to be free from governmental intrusion (protected by the Constitution) and the protection from intrusion into our private lives by others (protected by common law).

Private Key: A shared algorithm between all members of the same group; one key in a two-key pair.

Problem of anonymity: A person can claim to be anybody when creating a web page and putting information into it; there is no verification that you are who you claim.

Public Key: The second key in a two-key pair.

Public Key Infrastructure (PKI): System used for sending and receiving information without exposing it to unauthorized individuals.

Public Web: Anything on the Internet to which a search engine has access.

Ransomware: Malicious software inadvertently downloaded to a computer that subsequently locks the computer screen until an acceptable pass code is entered, usually after some sort of money transfer.

Reshipping: To receive packages at their residence and subsequently repackage the merchandise for shipment, usually abroad.

RFID: Radio frequency identification chips.

Risk: The potential for loss, damage, or destruction of an asset as a result of a threat exploiting a vulnerability.

Salting: Random data that is used as an additional input to a one-way function that "hashes" a password or passphrase.

Scope of Work: A legally binding and limiting component of a technical contract that specifies exactly what is to be accomplished, when, and with what standards of equipment.

SETI: Search for Extra-Terrestrial Intelligence.

Server: A computer program or a device that provides functionality for other programs or devices, called "clients."

Shared Key: A shared algorithm between all members of the same group.

Silk Road: An online narcotics-selling Tor network taken down by the US in 2013.

Software Vulnerabilities: The inherent and intentional or unintentional gaps in programing that allow outside programs to utilize or corrupt a system.

SPAM: Unsolicited bulk e-mail.

Spear-phishing: The fraudulent practice of sending e-mails ostensibly from a known or trusted sender in order to induce targeted individuals to reveal confidential information.

Spoofing: The dissemination of e-mail which is forged to appear as though it was sent by someone other than the actual source.

Streaming Encryption: Takes the "bit stream" and continuously encrypts data as it is prepared to be sent.

Symmetric Encryption: A form of computerized cryptography using a singular encryption key to guise an electronic message.

Terminal Mainframe Network: Computers used primarily by large organizations for critical applications, bulk data processing, such as census, industry and consumer statistics, enterprise resource planning, and transaction processing.

Theft: The physical removal of an object that is capable of being stolen without the consent of the owner and with the intention of depriving the owner of it permanently; the generic term for all crimes in which a person intentionally and fraudulently takes personal property of another without permission or consent and with the intent to convert it to the taker's use (including potential sale).

Threats: Anything that can exploit a vulnerability, intentionally or accidentally, and obtain, damage, or destroy an asset.

Tor: The Onion Router, an overlay network that operates on the public web, which uses increasing layers of encryption to make end-to-end web traffic anonymous.

Vulnerabilities: Weaknesses or gaps in a security program that can be exploited by threats to gain unauthorized access to an asset or assets.

Whitelist: A list of discrete entities, such as hosts or applications that are known to be benign and are approved for use within an organization and/or information system.

Wide Area Network: A computer network in which the computers connected may be far apart, generally having a radius of more than 1 km.

World Wide Web: An interconnected web of servers that simply switch packets of information around the globe.

INDEX

Printed in the USA
CPSIA information can be obtained
at www.ICGtesting.com
JSHW060910230224
57870JS00005B/33

9 781524 921965